A Century of Faces and Places

A History of Aldborough & Thurgarton 1900 - 2000

by
Keith Entwistle

Pictorial Maps
by
Geraldine Frances

Researched and published by
Aldborough Village History Society

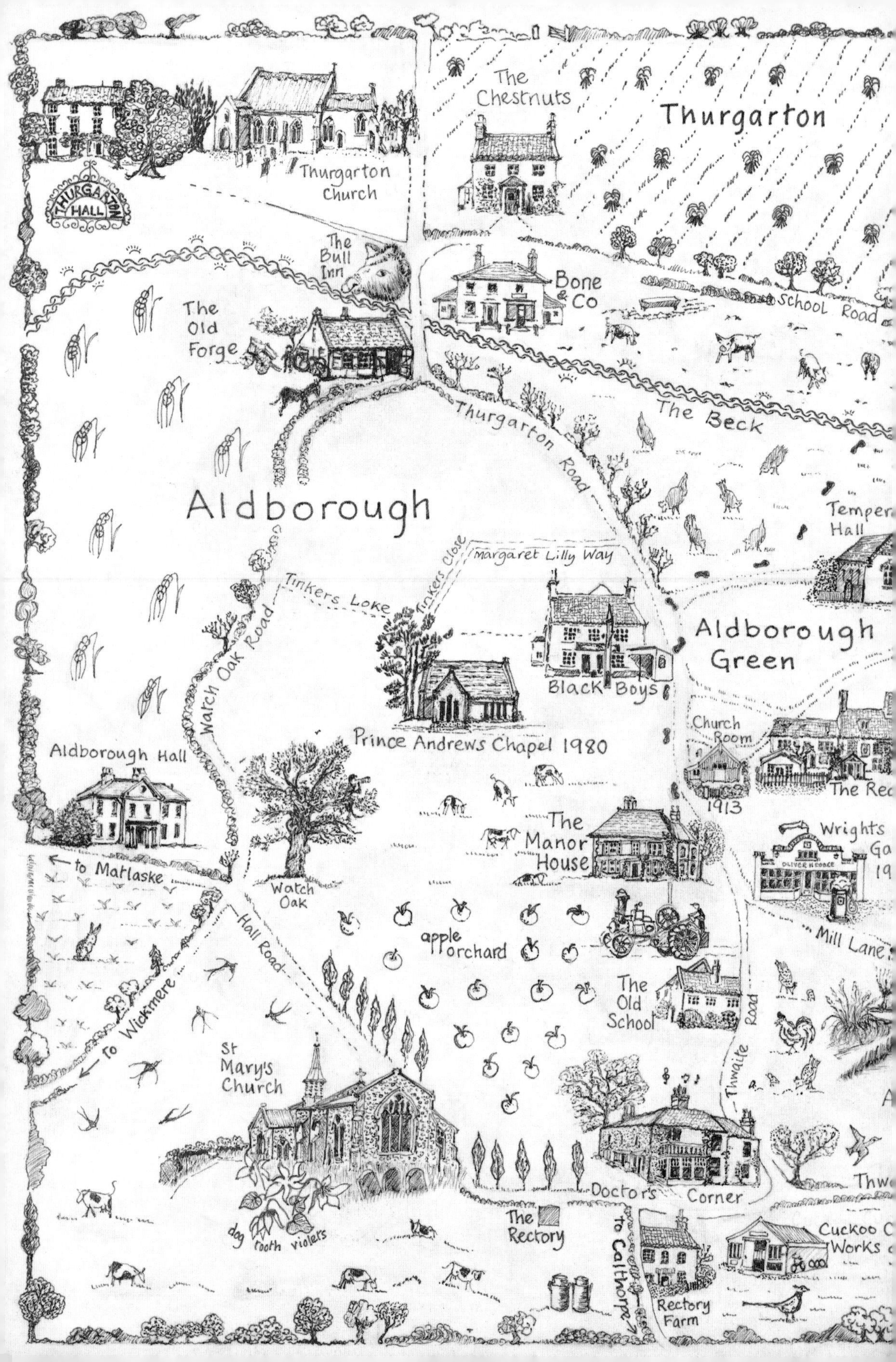

The Chestnuts
Thurgarton
THURGARTON HALL
Thurgarton Church
The Bull Inn
Bone & Co
School Road
The Old Forge
The Beck
Thurgarton Road
Aldborough
Temper
Hall
Margaret Lilly Way
Tinkers Close
Tinkers Loke
Watch Oak Road
Aldborough Green
Black Boys
Prince Andrews Chapel 1980
Church Room 1913
The Rec
Aldborough Hall
to Matlaske
The Manor House
Wrights
Ga
19
OLIVER H CODGE
Watch Oak
Mill Lane
Hall Road
apple orchard
The Old School
to Wickmere
Thwaite Road
St Mary's Church
Doctor's Corner
Thw
The Rectory
to Calthorpe
dog tooth violets
Cuckoo C
Works
Rectory Farm

A Pictorial Map of Aldborough & Thurgarton 1900 ~ 2000

Copyright © 2002 Aldborough Village History Society
c/o St Anne's Cottage
Aldborough
Norfolk NR11 7AA

First published in Great Britain in 2002
by Aldborough Village History Society
in association with
Brick Kiln Books

All rights reserved

No part of this publication may be reproduced, stored in a retrieval system, or transmitted, in any form or by any means without the prior written permission of the publisher, nor be otherwise circulated in any form of binding or cover other than that in which it is published and without a similar condition being imposed on the subsequent purchaser.

ISBN: 0 9543935 0 3

Typeset in Plantin and Gill
by Claire Knight

Printed and bound in Great Britain
by Broadgate Printers, Aylsham

This project has been supported by

AWARDS FOR ALL

This book is dedicated to the people of Aldborough and Thurgarton past and present.

Contents

A pictorial map of Aldborough &
Thurgarton 1900-2000   ii

Introduction   vi

The Early Years 1900-1920s   1

Before the Second World War 1920s-1939
     Part One   33
     Part Two   59

During the Second World War 1939-1945   81

The Middle Years 1945-1975   97

The Last Quarter 1975-2000   139

A pictorial map of Aldborough Green   160

Introduction

The following pages have come into being over a period of fifteen months. We started in July, 2001, after initial discussions had led to the founding of the Village History Society. Our first target was to gain enough material to hold an exhibition as part of Aldborough Village Show in early September. That established the project in the public mind; important contacts were made with former residents and with the families of former residents; local people who had come to the early meetings were now joined by a much wider group who were keen to be involved. Our primary objective from the outset was to publish our book in the autumn, 2002. And here we are!

By the end of 2001 an amazing volume of material had already been offered, in the form of photos, documents, diaries, letters, recollections. From the beginning we used the tape-recorded interview as a way of preserving information given by word of mouth. Memory is often a fragile faculty; in the right setting, and with the right prompts, it can return us to former decades with ease and speak of times and experiences long gone. It does not, however, operate to order, and it never travels in a straight line. In returning to the past it moves according to a pulse of feeling, it rarely follows a track of intention. We combined individual interviews with group sessions, where we explored particular topics such as school or places of worship, trades and businesses around the Green, cricket. And in the course of these, further topics were brought to the surface, quite unexpectedly. One particular session comes to mind: the stated topic was the Community Centre, but very quickly we had diverted to wonderful tales of the Youth Club, and the stirring exploits of the 'Tug-of-War boys'. Read all about them!

Gradually, then, the key events and people who created the story of Aldborough and Thurgarton began to emerge from the piles of documents and the hours of talk. Suddenly a photo would appear which brought a face to a story heard, a place to a recollection told. Links were seen between one person's story and another person's letter. A century of faces and places was beginning to acquire its own distinctive shape.

A process of exploration such as this, however, brings no guarantees. We cannot predetermine the content. Some topic areas are very full in source material, others are embarrassingly thin. Who would have predicted that the Red Lion and the Black Boys, not exactly the domain of the taciturn, would release such a minimal supply of stories? Perhaps the only conclusion is that either they are all unprintable, or that alcohol has a crippling effect on mental recall!

Think of this book as a print equivalent of a television documentary. It deals in personal versions of events, in eye-witness accounts; moreover, it presents these in the words actually used. I have deliberately tried to preserve in my tapescripts the rhythms of daily speech, where meaning can often dispense with grammar, and where vivid phrases can almost defy punctuation.

Finally, I should like to thank all who have contributed. I have heard every word spoken, I have read every document produced. Inevitably, I have had to make selections, and that process involves choosing here, but discarding there. My only hope is that the depth of my reading and listening has brought a necessary authority to my selections, and that I have exercised a fair judgment in any choice made. All of us who have worked on the production of this book hope that it proves an enjoyable and informative experience, bringing to us all, whether newcomer or old-timer, a deeper appreciation of the heritage of Aldborough and Thurgarton.

Author's note

Please note the significance of the following punctuation code in this volume:-
Jane Smith "In earlier years…" *denotes material taken from a spoken source.*
Jane Smith In earlier years… *denotes material taken from a written source.*

The Early Years
1900 - 1920s

Summer holidays at Aldborough Mill	2
Aldborough Green	4
Sport on the Green	6
Cricket	6
Bowls	7
Aldborough Fair	8
Robert Massingham, Carrier	11
General Traders	13
Days' shop	13
Bone & Co.	14
Kents' Shop.	14
Religion	15
Breakfast at the Mill	16
The School	17
Extracts from the School Log	18
The Opening of the New School	20
Water Gardens at Aldborough Mill	21
The Great Flood	24
Weddings	27
The First World War	28
Prisoners of War	30
Joe Hulls' Farewell	32

Summer Holidays at Aldborough Mill...

Let's join young Clifford Craske aboard the train now taking him to Aylsham station, in the year 1902. Or perhaps it is already 1909 - Clifford came every year of his boyhood, from a very early age until he was a young man, when the First World War broke the pattern of his holidays. But now he is about to start one of his regular summer visits to the old family home of his mother, born Anna Cooke, at Aldborough Mill. The route is already familiar to him and he knows who to expect on arrival.

In later life, Clifford wrote a memoir of these times, from which these extracts are taken.

I want to tell you about Aldborough Mill and the people who once lived there. No-one knew the exact age of the mill, but my mother was born there in 1850, when my grandfather had long been established as the miller. I was first taken to the mill at about the age of four, and at least once a year thereafter until old enough to go alone to stay, which I did very often, until the events which I shall describe caused the 'old home', as Mother called it, to be abandoned as a dwelling.

Aylsham was the nearest station, and my uncle Harry awaited us there with an old-fashioned four-wheeled vehicle of shabby appearance, drawn by an aged horse. My uncle was a bachelor of middle age, with a short grey beard and kindly eyes.

Clifford then talks about the religious and political beliefs which had occupied his uncle for much of his life, which made him remote and absent in more worldly affairs.

This passionate involvement had not, however, soured his nature, which was pleasant and peace-loving, but he cared little for his personal appearance, and the business of the mill came second to his political and religious activities. Worst of all, from the point of view of getting us home, he was of no use with a horse; and while humming some wordless hymn and meditating on far-off battles, he would let the reins bob limply up and down upon his knee, while the old horse jogged, walked, stopped and (on one occasion) sat down in the middle of the road, without any sort of direction from his master.

In the course of an hour or so, the journey was finished, and the whitened, weather-boarded walls of the mill peeped over the hedges across the flat, marshy meadows. My blind aunt Emily had long stood at the door, bonneted and shawled ready to welcome us. Embracing us all, she led us into the Passage, as the first room was called, where a noble meal was ready. In a dreamy, far-away manner, my uncle said grace, and we fell to.

We shall return to the mill shortly, but meantime we will make our way to Aldborough Green, and survey the scene that would greet a visitor in the early years of the century.

Aldborough Green

We will be looking at the individual buildings and their history later in this book, but for now let us read this general description as written by John Brown, a key figure in the day-to-day affairs of the community during the first part of the century, and whose house on the west side of the Green bears his name.

John Brown The village always has been and is now a centre of trade and social activity. As far back as 1840, it had its tradespeople of all descriptions - grocer, bakers, butchers, blacksmiths, tailors, shoemakers, doctor, schoolmaster, tanners, curriers, plumbers and glaziers, carpenters, saddlers and Public House (Black Boys). The Red Lion was only a beerhouse.

In 1884 its sports and pastimes were centred on the village green. Cricket was very much to the fore, having two or three county players living in the parish. The game of quoits was played outside both public houses. Skittles or ninepins were played at the pubs.

The Friendly Societies held their Annual Club Feast on the second Thursday in May. A Great Event. Members would meet at their respective lodges and don their regalia and meet on the Green. A band would be in attendance headed by two outriders dressed in Lincoln green, and the whole company would march to

HOLT DISTRICT.

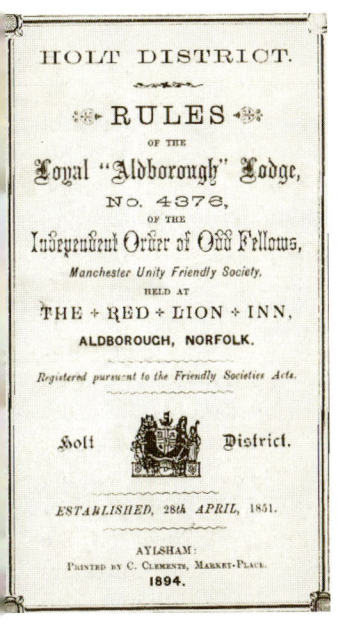

RULES
OF THE
Loyal "Aldborough" Lodge,
No. 4878,
OF THE
Independent Order of Odd Fellows,
Manchester Unity Friendly Society,
HELD AT
THE ✛ RED ✛ LION ✛ INN,
ALDBOROUGH, NORFOLK.

Registered pursuant to the Friendly Societies Acts.

Holt   District.

ESTABLISHED, 28th APRIL, 1851.

AYLSHAM:
PRINTED BY C. CLEMENTS, MARKET-PLACE.
1894.

church with banners flying; and after the service they would all go to their lodges and sit down to roast beef, dumplings and plum puddings and plenty of ale. Following, there would be sports on the Green. Races for cycles, the pennyfarthing model, flat races for all-comers and various other competitions. A small fair would be on the Green for the event and so would end an excitable day.

In those far-off days we were isolated to a very great extent, the only public conveyance being a carrier's van which came through the village to and from Norwich on Wednesdays and Saturdays, a far cry from present day conditions with three 26 seater buses, taxis and private cars. Until 1886, the nearest telegraph office was at Hanworth; after that date the line was brought to Aldborough. Until 1886 our letters came from Hanworth, the postman riding on horseback. The present post office is the third that the writer remembers in the village.

There was not much excitement for the rest of the year, Valentine's day for children, harvest frolics and bonfire night when nothing burnable must be left lying about. (The ancient village stocks which used to stand on the Green were destroyed at one of the bonfires.) The opening of a one-day bank came to the village in 1893. We paid 2d a week for education till the Free Education Act was passed. The population of the village has grown but little through the years; in 1841 it stood at 293 and in 1931 it was 295.

5

Sport on the Green

Cricket

He mentioned cricket! This has clearly been a key feature of village life for a very long time. The earliest photographic evidence we have is this photo taken, we understand, about 1880. Research in county records reveals that Aldborough Cricket Club is one of the oldest in Norfolk, having played on the Green for over 160 years, except for 1914-18, and 1939-45. According to the WI History,

Aldborough has played cricket on the Green every summer for very many years, and tales of the mighty hits of the 'good old days' are still told. The shops used to put up shutters to protect their windows. The Revd A.C. Davies, Rector in 1882, had played for Sussex before he played for Aldborough. Mr Sam Tolman, who was formerly on the Ground Staff at Fenners, played for the club for some years, and died on the field during a match in 1929. Of late years, with fewer animals grazing on the Green, the grass has grown up and the pitch has deteriorated.

We cannot name any of the players in this photo; however, the club has in its possession a letter (written in 1949) from a sprightly 88 year old,

Mr G.H. Quint who played for Buxton, against Aldborough, in 1887. His memory of the game 60 years before is very sharp, and no wonder. He writes:

Mr G. H. Quint Batting first, you could total only 71. I was the chief cause of the small score as I took eight wickets. Buxton scored 242 thanks to Revd Wickham (wicket-keeper for the county) and Tindell (a Cambridge blue). Your parson was the most successful bowler.

He goes on to list the 1887 team, and it is likely that some of the players were involved a few years earlier.

Team list: Revd A.C. Davies, R. Legge, Wilson, J.H. Spurrell, W. Spurrell, Amis, B. Oakley, J.M. Hulls, B. Stanton, Burgess, Pucken.

Note a certain J.M. Hulls… we get to know him later! But there were hazards faced by those players…

Ida Impson "There used to be two ponds on the Green, what they called the Big Pit and the Little Pit. The Big Pit was more or less in the middle of the Green, and the little one was nearly opposite the Stone House where I was born; when there was a very sharp frost, we used to skate on them… when they had cricket matches on the Green, you see, some batsmen hit the ball hard, and that went off the edge, over the brow of the hill, and into one of the ponds."

…and hazards faced by the spectators, too!

Audrey Day "Old Willy Pye, do you remember him? Was he the one sitting watching the cricket when an old bird did something in his pipe? Father Day used to put forms out in front of the old warehouse; old men used to sit and watch the cricket, and there was an old blackbird that come and **** in his pipe! "Dirty old bitch," he said. *(Peals of laughter)* Needless to say, he never forgot that! Those are the sort of things you remember, and what you want to remember, you don't!"

Bowls

Aldborough bowling green was situated between The Red Lion and the Church Room.

The newspaper announcement of the death of Mr W. Spurgeon includes this statement: 'For many years he was Captain of the Cricket Club… as a bowl player he ranked among the best in Norfolk, and he was at his death Captain of the Aldborough Bowling Club.'

Aldborough Fair

The major annual event associated with Aldborough is, of course, the Fair. We know that the original charter was granted by King John, and that it has taken place, in some shape or form, ever since. During the First World War, for example, the tradition was maintained through the presence of a lone stall-holder.

Cynthia Greene "Now you know that was a chartered fair, don't you? Well now, you see, during the First World War, if nobody had come, they could have done away with it, so there was a Rock King - I can see that stall as if that was yesterday; he used to come there for two days especially to keep that a chartered fair."

John Brown now describes the scene in the early years of the century.

The fair was the next event. For well over one hundred years, the fair has been a great attraction for the village and the surrounding countryside. Its stock fair on June 21st drew large crowds of farmers and workers from a wide area. Men on the farms would be at work at 4 o'clock in the morning in the hay harvest till 8 o'clock and then dress in their Sunday best and off to the fair.

The stock fair consisted of fat and store cattle, sheep and pigs (auctioneers Messrs Irelands). Mine host J. Wilkin of the Red Lion supplied the cattle pens. The pens for the sheep and pigs were supplied by the auctioneers.

The sale over the horse fair began with a great deal of trotting up and down and then chasing round the Green to try out their mettle. The pleasure fair would begin late afternoon on the 21st. The Green would be fairly covered with stalls, showbooths for boxing and conjuring. There would be large booths for the general public. One large booth, placed on the north end of the Green, would be called the Temperance Booth where minerals and food were sold. In the same booth on the second fair morning a free breakfast would be provided for all the van dwellers and their families. Funds were provided by ladies and gentlemen outside the village. By noon on the second day the fair would begin in earnest, women and children from the surrounding villages would attend.

There would be roundabouts. The first the writer remembers were pushed around from inside and we boys would take part and have a free ride for our services, and then came those with pony attached and we lost our free rides. Then came the real steam-horses which were very grand, lit up at night by the old oil flares. There would be cheapjacks, men dancing on hot irons, sword swallowers, Wild West shows etc. and so ended the chief event of the year.

The fair did not pass off too smoothly as there would be free-fights as most of the outstanding quarrels of the local fairs were settled at Aldborough this being the last local fair of the year. There would be occasional quarrels among the van dwellers, the writer having seen living vans turned over with people in them and a good deal of rough play.

Aldborough fair time was a time for local feasting with beef, plum pudding and new potatoes.

The WI History has this to say:

In days gone by, all kinds of wares were sold on this occasion, and there were horse, livestock and poultry sales, as well as the traditional hiring of servants. The fair was started by the oldest inhabitants playing a match of tipcat on the Green.

Villagers remember the fair in their early days.

Anthony Day "I used to have a shilling the time the fair got there to spend, that's all. You could ride on any of them things for a penny or tuppence, couldn't you; cake-walk and that, that was only a penny.

The horse-trading on the Green... I can remember Mother putting a chair in our hall down the Stone House, sitting me on that, I used to watch all these old dealers going around the Green like mad with their horses; I had a little sailor-suit, I can remember that... they had swingboats, and of course the old traction engines used to run the steam-horses and all that, they were good old days really, coconut shies and darts, hitting a thing with a hammer and ringing a bell, the old punchbag, cakewalk, steam-horses - there used to be two steam-horses; old Dack had steam-horses, Kenny Wright had steam-horses; a man name of Thurston used to come with Gondolas, used to stand them up there near the Black Boys. There used to be rock stalls - they used to spit in it! - (peals of laughter). They'd come to the shop to buy extra sugar - they were good for the trade, the fair people were, oh yes. There was an old man Hamlyn lived in one of father's houses; he used to go down Kents' Loke and dig up potatoes for the fair people, used to sell all his 'taters to them! Kenny Gray and Dack used to have a traction engine - fair engines we used to call them, they were different, they had a good old dynamo on the front."

Members of the Gray family who brought the fair to Aldborough throughout the twentieth century, except for during the two World Wars.

Cynthia Greene "When Aldborough Fair was on, they used to go from one pub to the other, 'cos my mother used to cry, they used to put as many men into a cart as they could get and more, and whip those ponies, and go from Aldborough Black Boys to Thurgarton Bull. The first fair morning, we were never allowed to go out to our music lessons or anything, we weren't allowed outside the door, you know, that was a horse-fair, they used to whip them, my mother used to get so upset. Those men used to hang on the carts, 'cos they'd had too much to drink."

Ida Impson "June 21 and 22 were what was called Official Clear Days, no matter what day it came... in my very early days, all the people with the fair came with horse-drawn vehicles and vans; and there used to be one they called the big steam-horses on the Green, and a little one *(steam-horse ride)* for the children to ride; they had to have a constant supply of water, and an old chap who was very lame used to come with a horse-drawn tub on wheels and come down just off the Green to the bridge to get pails of water into the tub and take back."

Her brother, Albert Massingham, recalls these scenes in a letter to his grandchildren.

Albert Massingham "When we lived on the Green our house had a splendid view of the fair, this was a highlight in our calendar, it meant time off from school and money to spend! The fairground people would set up their stalls and roundabouts which suited the young folk very well but for the older people the horse trading was of importance. The horse dealers would import New Forest and

Welsh ponies all young animals to be sold on the first fair day and the Green would be a very busy place indeed. The publican from the Red Lion would set up his beer tent to cater for the very thirsty public, he would sell bottled mild beer, doubtless this was a very good day for him."

Bertram Gray
Albert Gray
Alfie Hart
Kenneth Gray (Driver)

We now turn our attention to some of the businesses active in the early years of the century.

Robert Massingham, Carrier

John Brown mentioned the carrier's van which made a twice-weekly visit to Norwich. It was owned and driven by Robert Massingham. His son Albert and daughter Ida recall these times.

Ida Impson "I was born in the Stone House on Aldborough Green, quite close to the little village shop, the name over the shop was Day. There was no room for stables or anything of that kind, so father's horses and van stood at Thurgarton Bull, which was a public house as you go into Thurgarton. Later on, we moved from that Stone House on the Green into another house which they partly re-built just off the end of the Green; and a big 'van-house' (as it was called then) was built, so father was then able to have his van standing there. There was a stable for three horses, and the end of that was the hay-house, as we called it."

Albert also wrote about his own father to his grand-children.

Albert Massingham "Each Wednesday and Saturday, my father, Robert Massingham, would go to Norwich, taking both goods and passengers to the city. Sometimes I would go with him and when we reached Norwich he would park the carrier's cart and stable the horses at a pub called the Duke's Palace. I would deliver packages in the city and collect up others for us to take back to Aldborough, Matlaske, Wickmere, Itteringham, Erpingham and many other places… During the First World War my father used two Army mules - I believe their names were Peter and Tom - and these were hired out to him under the 'meat for manners' arrangement. That means that the animals were used for working purposes and my father did not have to pay the Army for the work they did but stabled and fed them."

Cynthia Greene remembers those mules.

Cynthia Greene "Ida Impson's father, he had an old covered van with two mules, and he used to go to Norwich twice a week; now those mules, well, it took six men to push them to make them start in the mornings - they never would go! I can see the people pushing them now, pushing the cart behind. They wouldn't move! And Ida used to lay her head by the beck, going down to where the chapel was, she used to lay her ear on there, and she could hear him coming over Calthorpe bridge. He had an old lorry in the finish, that was always breaking down…."

Anthony Day remembers the mules, too!

Anthony Day "Old Bob Massingham used to have a couple of mules which he used to take to Norwich with an old covered sort of wagon. He'd have a packet of margarine out of somebody's box when he wanted to grease his wheels!" *(peals of laughter)*

And another story about Bob the carrier.

Cynthia Greene "My father used to tell a tale about a poacher who was on Bob Massingham's van; he got in a box in there and the police were sitting on the top of it looking for him, 'cos he was a poacher, and he rode to Norwich with the police sitting on top of the thing!"

The man holding the horse is John Brown, brother-in-law to Bertie Day, who is standing by the shop-door with his mother.

Bertie Day

General Traders

Days' Shop

The Stone House is where the Massingham family lived for a while, and it was next door that Days' shop started trading.

Anthony Day "My father's shop started in 1901; he had previously worked for Bone & Co. He got married 1903 and my brother Bert was born 1904, down in the Stone House; father lived there then, but he moved out of there, and into Chesterfield House, where my brother George, Ada, Hally and me were all born there; then, when I was about 2 years old, father moved down to Stone House, and he kept in there right till his time. He bought it in 1913. I remember when he bought Orchard House from Mrs Durrant; after she died, her nephew asked Father if he wanted to buy it. Father said, "Yes, I will. How much do you want?" He told him, my father went upstairs and got the money and paid, just like that! That was the finish of it, wasn't no deeds or nothin', I don't think, hardly anything else, all the money was under the bed or somewhere."

*The **Bone & Co.** property was originally 3 buildings, later joined, and constantly altered, dating from the 16th century. Bone & Co. began with groceries, later developing into a General Store selling a wide range of goods that included ironmongery, drapery, oil, paraffin, toys, linen, shoes, lino, clothes etc. There was a delivery and collection service by horse and cart, each with a man and a boy.*

Bone & Co.

The "Old Thatched Shop" was bought in 1833 by John Bone. Previously it had been called "The Cook and Key".

W.I. History At about 3am one night in March 1920 the harness room at Bone's was gutted by a fire which was well advanced before it was discovered. There were 8 horses stabled alongside and their halters were quickly cut to free them. Everyone rushed out to safety.

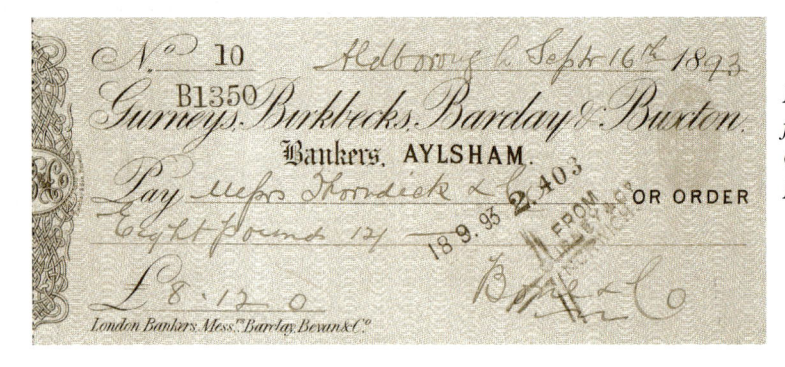

Note the names of the families who formed the banking syndicate. Gurney, Birkbeck, Barclay and Buxton.

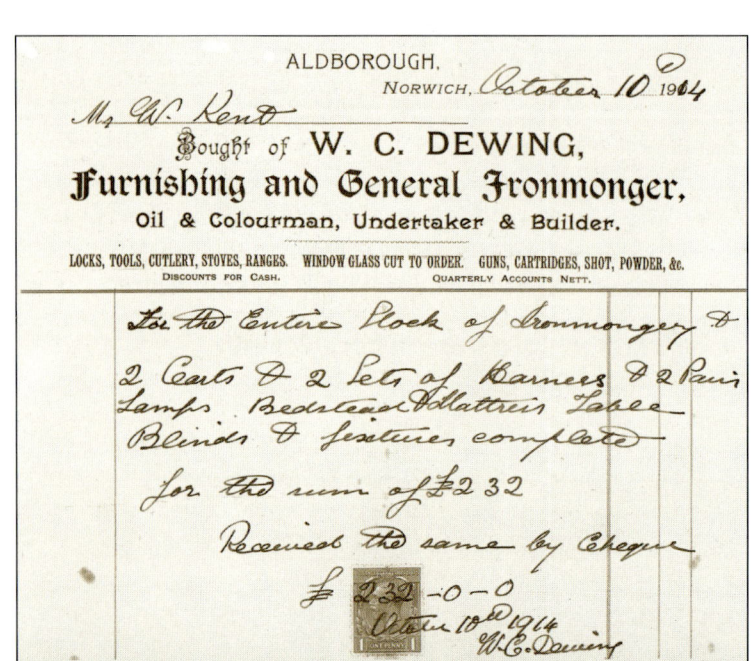

Kents' Shop

There was sufficient business for three general traders based on Aldborough Green to prosper for nearly seventy years of the twentieth century. Indeed, Bone & Co. proved to be a sound training base for the other two; both Days' and Kents' were founded by former Bone employees.

William Kent took over the premises formerly run by the Dewing family in 1914. Here is his receipt for the purchase of the business.

Religion

The Dewings played another key role in village life, in combining with others to build the new Methodist Chapel.

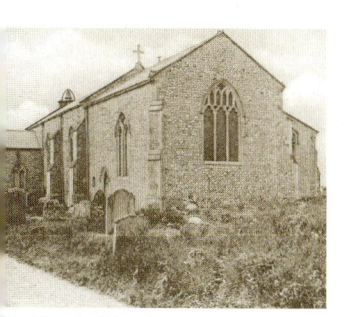

The chapel minutes, lodged in the Record Office in Norwich, reveal the following information.

Notes Land in Thurgarton was purchased from Frederick King; Mr Chestney and Mr Dewing obtained an estimate of £510 for building of the new chapel, and moves were made to raise the money, in particular, "permission to solicit gentlemen to lay foundation stones, the amount to be laid on each stone to be £5 and upwards".

Over £100 was raised by this and other means, and the shortfall was made up by selling off the old chapel for £40, and obtaining a loan of £400 from Barclays Bank. Stones were laid on 25 September, 1907 and 24 October, and the new chapel was opened on 17 May, 1908, with a public meeting and tea. The loan was to prove a major burden for many years - the WI History records fund-raising efforts to pay the remaining sums off nearly forty years later!

These early years of the century saw a flurry of improvements to buildings for the various congregations. In 1906, the turret was added to St Mary's, and a few years later, in 1913, the Parish Room (soon called the Church Room) was built on land to the end of the garden to the Red Lion (where the Bowling Green was located). This church property was largely the initiative of the Gay family of Aldborough Hall, and would prove to be a magnificent focus for community activity in succeeding decades. We can take a glimpse at the day it was opened through the diary kept by Mrs Gay.

July 16, 1913 Bone's cart came a little before 10, and we got into it the piano, 3 trestle tables, the piano stool, and either on it or in the motor 60 cups and saucers, 60 tumblers… also our flags. Chris, Margaret and I went with them, and on the way picked up Mr and Mrs Borlase *(Mr Borlase was the Rector)* and we all went to the Parish Room. Mr Reynolds had also sent flags, and we decorated the room very prettily, with the help of Edmund and Daisy who joined up. The man came and tuned the piano, and the chairs from Norwich came while we were there. We came back for luncheon, and after motored back again for the opening ceremony at 3.30, taking the baskets of cakes with us. The ceremony began with Mr Borlase reading 2 or 3 collects *(prayers)*, and then making a speech about the object of the room, thanking all the helpers and stating the financial position. Then I declared the room opened, Dr Spurrell made a speech thanking me, and Edmund one returning thanks. There seemed to be 30 or 40 people present.

Meanwhile, a few years earlier in 1906, the building affectionately known as the Tin Tabernacle (replaced in 1980 by Prince Andrew's Chapel) was built, just off the Green, by the group of 'independent' believers to which the Cooke family belonged. Which brings us back to the young Clifford Craske and his holidays with his mother's family at Aldborough Mill, where a pious breakfast began the day.

St. Mary's Church

Mrs Gay

Breakfast at the Mill

Clifford Craske My grandfather, who died about 1899, was no longer active in the mill when I began my visits. I associated him with God, on account of his great age, long white beard, and venerable appearance. He presided till the end of his life over family prayers, held every morning before breakfast in the Parlour, a very beautiful old room that was entered from the Passage. If the whole family happened to be in residence, the room was packed; there were my uncles, Harry, Tom and William; my aunts Emily, Maria, Jane and Hannah, cousin John Lemmon, the Companion, my parents and myself. There were usually two domestic servants at the mill and these came in and stood by the door.

My grandfather read a passage from the Bible, then said, "Let us pray", whereupon we all knelt down beside our chairs. My father, who was short and stout, assumed this position with reluctance, and maintained it with difficulty; possibly his thoughts, like mine, were fixed on the excellent round of ham that always appeared upon the breakfast table.

There was a chamber organ with a rosewood case and golden pipes, and a piano with green silk behind a fretwork front. But we did not sing until the evening; then my uncle Tom Cooke would play the violin on which he was a very good performer, my father played the piano, and sometimes - a great treat for us - my uncle Tom Craske - would come over from Holt and play the organ. And so with music and reading aloud, we would spend many an hour when darkness fell, our only light the great oil lamp standing by the latticed window. The bookshelves were full of interest and contained many rare and beautiful volumes.

He carries on with a detailed description of the house and outbuildings, (which we shall sadly have to omit), continuing with this introduction to the garden - important to our story.

There was a beautiful kitchen garden, where the finest fruit bushes were grown under a closely netted enclosure. Following a path which ran along the bank of a small branch of the millstream, you went on to discover a rustic bridge leading to another garden, where in the month of June, you were welcome to raise the netting over some of the finest strawberries in Norfolk. There was also in this garden, which was surrounded by tall shrubs, a summerhouse which, I daresay, could have told its tale, for it was far away from the mill, and took some finding.

Near this garden was a large and level field, just right for football; indeed it was the scene of many a game between the village lads whom my uncle Harry loved to befriend and have around him.

The School

No doubt many of the boys who played football on Henry Cooke's field were pupils at the School - which certainly didn't have a sports field at its disposal. Albert Massingham started his schooling there.

Albert Massingham "My schooldays started in the old village school, this became a private house when the Norfolk County Council built the school now in use and when I was about nine or ten years old I transferred to the new school. Our schoolmaster's name was Mr Joseph Hulls, a very strict man indeed but a fair one who demanded respect from his pupils and if it was not forthcoming he would know the reason why. Another of our teachers was a Miss Rose Earl, she was very popular with the children, perhaps because she herself had been a pupil at the school before she became a teacher."

Albert's comments - after an interval of 70 years or so - guide our own look at the school in the early years of the century. We have had access to the log-books as from 1865, and we may pick up references to the two names he mentions as from 1885, the date of the appointment as Head Master one Joseph Millington Hulls. (He has already featured as a member of the 1887 cricket team.) And in due course we will have good cause to remember, too, the name of Rose Earl…

So far in these pages, we have taken rather a privileged look at life in Aldborough and Thurgarton - holidays, and special days - but now we turn to harsher aspects of everyday life, conditions at the village school. Until 1907, this was housed in a building now known as Old School Cottages, just off the road to the left between Doctor's Corner and Manor Farm. There follows a selection of Joseph Hulls' entries from the school log for the early years of the century. These have been chosen to illustrate certain key aspects of life at school as perceived by the Head Master: frequent poor health of the children, cramped and miserable facilities for teaching, the effect of bad weather on attendance, priority given at certain times of year to work on the farm (e.g. harvest) and inadequate staffing levels. But throughout, he battles for improvements.

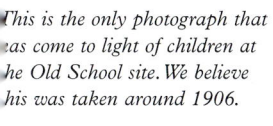

This is the only photograph that has come to light of children at the Old School site. We believe this was taken around 1906.

Pictured overleaf:
View looking down towards the road from the former school building, soon after conversion into cottages

Extracts from school log
Mixed School
Discipline is satisfactory, and very creditable standard is reached in instruction. The appearance of the interior has been improved, but improvement in general tidiness must still be looked for.

October 18, 1900 Number on books: 101 average for week 73.3%. The Ropers have not yet returned, and I am now informed that the doctor has forbidden them to come back. It seems that they have some comparatively trifling but very contagious and unpleasant complaint, which should be cured in 3 or 4 days. The doctor, however, says that the treatment recommended has not been followed. It appears to me like a carefully calculated evasion of the Act. Another small boy, Humphreys, is away with scarlet fever, and I have, for the present, refused to admit children from Matlaske, who have been living next door to a case in that village.

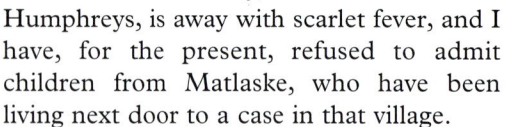

October 11, 1901 Attendance very low during week; many children have colds, while several have bad sore throats. Last evening a little girl (Marten) died from diphtheria, and I have therefore excluded the Culleys (3) and Martens (4), pending instructions from the Medical Officer of Health. I have also received notice from Dr Spurrell that C. Perkins has diphtheria, and I shall exclude both him and his sister. Dr Spurrell also recommends the exclusion of every child who shows any sign of sore throat.

June 12, 1902 With regard to closets mentioned in His Majesty's Inspector's (HMI) report, I have examined them carefully since. The girls' closets (3) were by far the more offensive, so far as regards smell. Beyond this, there was little to complain of in two of them; in the third the seat was very wet. This is due, I find, to the absence of a urinal for the small boys, an omission which, somewhat strangely, never occurred to me before. I have arranged, however, that the omission shall be immediately remedied.

October 3, 1902 Re-opened school after 5 weeks holiday, the original month having been extended in consequence of slow harvest; even now, harvest is by no means complete. The work during the week has resolved itself as usual into finding how little the children remember of the previous eight months' work.

October 23, 1903 Infants very crowded. Plans have been at Board of Education for some time for enlargement as suggested by the HMI. Number on books, 113.

February 2, 1904 The Infants room is overcrowded; considering the want of space, the children are well managed and fairly taught. The staff should be at once strengthened to meet the requirements of Art. 73 of the Provisional Code, which are not at present satisfied.

March 18, 1904 Attendance very bad, much sickness. Admitted 6 children from Thwaite... the worst feature, however, is that the children seem to have no habit of study; left to themselves they merely stare about.

March 24, 1904 During this week there has been rapid spread of whooping cough, a few cases of which have been noted in the last three weeks. So general has it become, however, this week, that Doctor Spurrell advised the speedy closure of the school. It was therefore closed on Thursday afternoon until further notice.

October 14, 1904 I have tested the four fresh children from Hanworth. Generally they are willing enough, but their knowledge of general work is very small, their writing is lamentable, and also spelling and composition, and needlework. Of grammar, drill, history, geography, they know nothing. The worst feature about them is the sullenness of the girls, more especially. We are singularly free from this with our own children, and probably association or other means will eventually correct it.

January 19, 1905 School closed for council enquiry as to site for proposed new school building.

January 24, 1905 Report "The school is in a creditable state of efficiency, in spite of trying circumstances. The premises are cramped, the desks unsuitable and the staff inadequate, the Master being directly responsible for instruction of Standards ii to vii inclusive. Besides this, the attendance has been remarkably fluctuating on account of sickness."

February 4, 1905 No. on books, 134. I have this week received a fairly adequate supply of towels. Somewhat over a year ago I requisitioned what I considered enough; I was allowed two, one to use while the other was washed, which meant one towel for one week for 130 odd children. We now have a dozen, which permits a change on alternate days.

July 21, 1905 Attendance very poor, average 99, no. on books, 131. Several children away with sore throats or other minor complaints. This is a common occurrence after long spells of dry weather, followed by a heavy rain. I have for years attributed it to the following cause, which in my opinion is of such importance that it should be accurately recorded and noted from time to time, either to confirm the theory or to contradict it. The wells around here are all, or nearly all, shallow or surface wells, wells from which the water is drawn by ordinary pump; there are no draw wells. The ground in the long periods of drought is fouled on its surface by vegetable garbage and by the incidental throwing out of slops of various sorts in the close vicinity of the wells and houses. When the rain comes, these are washed into the wells, with the inevitable result that fouled water, probably drunk in large quantities because of the heat, lowered vitality which appears incidentally in the form of sore throats. I may say that I have noted the recurrence of these year after year.

July 4, 1906 Today a Committee Meeting was held at which I called the attention of the managers to the following matters.

1. HM Inspectors report on the dirtiness of the walls and the offensive smells from the office.
2. The condition of the urinals.
3. The inadequacy of the staff.
4. The overcrowding of the Infant room (42 children in a room 19'6" x 14'6").
5. The necessity for cleaning of troughs.
6. The need for water tub in girls' playground.
7. The flooding of lobbies by stormwater after every heavy rain, leaving behind a thick deposit of black mud.
8. Broken gate of playground.
9. Provision of curtains and rings for partial separation of classes in main room.
10. Necessity for gravelling of girls' playground.

September 15, 1906 Miss Earl away this week unwell.

September 22, 1906 (New pupils) are progressing and are at any rate getting to find that every answer is not to be found by a mixture of indiscriminate guess and gazing at the ceiling.

General report for 1906 Progress has been well maintained under the most unfavourable circumstances. From March 1 to April 27, the school was closed for measles, and on return of children I found it necessary to absolutely re-commence the work of the year. After this, good progress was made, but this was hindered very much by absences of teachers, owing to sickness. Miss Earl was seriously ill after harvest, and was unable to return to school until just before Xmas... the overcrowded state of the school, too, hinders really effective working. During the year the Infant room, 19'6" by 14'3" has frequently had 47 children in it, while every desk in the upper room has been full.

Copy of report of HMI following visit on December 3rd, 1906

Attention is directed to the last report. The delay in proceeding with the proposed new school makes it the more important that the classroom which is crowded with Infants should be cleaned at once, and the walls colour-washed. The surface of the playground is in such a state that it is not possible for the regular physical exercise to be taken out of doors.

February 8, 1907 I have reported the following matters to the managers.

Lobby again flooded. Condition of the playground and parks, drill has been impossible for weeks. Chimney in main room coming away from wall, with consequence that the slightest down-draught causes a rush of smoke into room. Miss Earl unwell since Tuesday. The influenza from which she suffered has left her very weak, and the slightest change affects her seriously. Attendance very poor, especially in Infant Room, many of the children being ill. Average for week, 113. No. on books, 141.

September 20, 1907 Holiday extended for one week, harvest being slow. Miss Hilda Smith began work with infants, Miss Earl having been granted three months holiday by the Education Committee.

October 12, 1907 This morning I read instructions from Mr Bushell to vacate the school by Friday, as the tenancy of the old school and house terminates on that date...

So deeply needed, so long awaited, the new school building located just over the parish boundary at Alby brought frustrations in the early weeks after opening that must have been deeply trying to Mr Hulls and his staff.

Week ending 18 October

This morning I came prepared to open school, but I found it in such a generally unclean condition that I did not open. The play-ground was a mud pool; in the school-rooms, no attempt had been made to sweep up the accumulated mud and dirt incidental to the moving. The desks were as muddy as they could be, considering they had been moved in the wet and mud of last week. I sent to the chairman asking him to call round to see the conditions, but he did not come. No provision has been made for school-cleaning, and no school cleaner appears to have been appointed. Mr Herbert Cook, one of the managers came round, however, and I directed his attention to the matter.

On Tuesday afternoon we opened school. There are no chairs, one cupboard, no shelves, no hooks from which to suspend maps, and in consequence of the paucity of the manifestly unfit desks about thirty-five children have during the week been sitting

The opening of the new school, 1907

on the floor. The condition of the playground is as last week. The entrance is a pool of clay in which the feet sink ankle-deep. There is no division between the boys' and girls' offices, and in every way the position is lamentable.

Thursday Today Mr Key HMI visited and I pointed out to him various errors of construction and numerous deficiencies. The supply of drinking water is limited to a soft water supply, the drain from which carries the waste water back into the supply tank.

Week ending October 25

The comments of last week may be repeated, though in consequence of my complaints and suggestions some outside alterations have been made. Result of week's work very unsatisfactory, as might be expected.

November 1, 1907 I have this week learned that all things requisitioned have been passed by the Education Committee.

Conditions as last week. No drinking water has yet been supplied for the children beyond the ordinary soft water supply from a tank which must have been considerably fouled by the return of water which had been used for ablutionary purposes.

November 8, 1907 No supplies yet to hand; conditions as before in every way.

November 15, 1907 Conditions as reported last week.

November 22, 1907 On Wednesday the managers held a meeting and decided to summarily close the school. I was instructed accordingly. The resolution passed unanimously as I understand, was that "As the school and premises are unfit to receive the children, the managers have decided to close the school forthwith."

So a month of struggling on in the face of 'errors of construction and numerous deficiencies' resulted, eventually, in a decisive stand. They closed the school! It was the only way the School Managers had to force the Norfolk Education Committee to take notice. They were ordered to re-open within the week, but improvements were set in motion, even if they happened at a rate that was frustratingly slow to Joe Hulls.

Water Gardens at Aldborough Mill

In Clifford's account of his holidays at the mill, he writes, "Every summer brought flocks of human starlings from far and wide. Hungry nonconformist ministers coming for the "May Meetings", Liberals for a political rally, temperance orators, fishermen, naturalists eager to study the rare plants on the millstream islands, and the rare birds that made the place a sanctuary, all were welcomed round the table." What exactly did they come to see?

Looking at the mill site as it now is, with the original buildings converted to three homes, and with the other houses built nearby, it is difficult to imagine the area as it appeared in the early years of the century. But it is clear that Henry Cooke (Uncle Harry) had taken the wet environs of his working mill as the starting-point for the creation of water gardens that were a delight to all those who came to see and enjoy them. Little Cynthia from Colman's Corner remembers them.

Cynthia Greene "Aldborough Mill - my father's brother drove a 'four-in-hand' from

Cromer, they used to bring Sunday School treats for the day to Aldborough Mill, 'cos you remember when that was a lovely island, don't you? Children and parents, they'd come for the day... there were lovely little rustic bridges, they had punts and boats and everything - that's all filled up now. And they used to baptise people there, do you remember that? Used to dip them, didn't they? There was a beautiful old house there, the Cookes' house, that was all turned into the mill, that was a lovely place. It gradually deteriorated..."

And another memory.

Albert Massingham "Aldborough Mill was important in the life of the village, not only did people work there but as children we used to have Sunday School Treats and other parties on the mill meadow and we were all given a trip up the river in a rowing boat. The mill was in the possession of the Cooke family for many years, certainly from the early 1800s and Mr Henry Cooke was a keen gardener and I believe he was largely responsible for the planting of the island in the mill pond with flowers and bulbs. For many years the island was very lovely, especially in springtime with daffodils in bloom and both swans and ducks lived on the pond. Alas, now it is all a miserable mass of weeds and the mill no longer used for its original purposes."

Using a large-scale contemporary map, and looking carefully at photos that survive, we have created the following ground plan of the mill and its waterways as best we may.

The water-wheel gave unexpected opportunities for daredevils.

Gwen Coghlan "That was the terrible part to me, watching that wheel go round… my mother (née Cooke) used to get in there and hold on to that wheel, and go round with it… She'd go in there when she was about seventeen, she'd grasp the wheel - she was so daring - she'd go in there with the wheel - it was a huge thing. To reach it, you went inside the double doors, where all the clattering was, you went through, and down the passage, you could open these flaps and watch this huge thing go round, she'd climb down into the middle of it…"

An overall impression of the mill pond and environs with locations of buildings identified in our researches

Here is a further description of the area, as recalled by Clifford Craske.

"Looking at the photograph, you will see the broad expanse of the millstream, with one of its islands; and the boathouse, half-hidden among the trees and reeds. This island, which might almost have been enchanted, was crossed by little waterways that were spanned by bridges built by my Uncle Tom from fallen trees, gay with flowers, and alive at early morning with the song of birds. There was a boat and a canoe each in excellent repair, for my Uncle Harry was an enthusiastic and capable man with a pair of oars or a paddle. Learning from him, I was soon able to take either of these craft as far as the stream was navigable.

When on the water, my uncle Harry became dreamy and contemplative, forgetting the political and religious disputes of the day and the battles of the past. He would discourse with wide knowledge upon the peaceful country through which we glided. He was also interested in games for his boys; and at his request I drew up for him a simplified set of rules for association football, so that he could referee the matches in the field behind the mill. He was also a keen cricketer, taking an active part in matches on the village green; but his greatest interest was in the rare birds and plants of the islands, which even great naturalists like Cherry Kearton had come to study.

People of distinction in every walk of life visited the mill. Sir Henry Irving was one; and although my relations with their Puritan ancestry mistrusted the stage, they had received him hospitably. All the great preachers of the day were entertained, and many prominent politicians. Had there been such a thing as motor transport, the number of sightseers would have been even greater; but my Uncle Harry would not have enjoyed such publicity, being shy and retiring except when roused to do battle for nonconformity or the Liberal party."

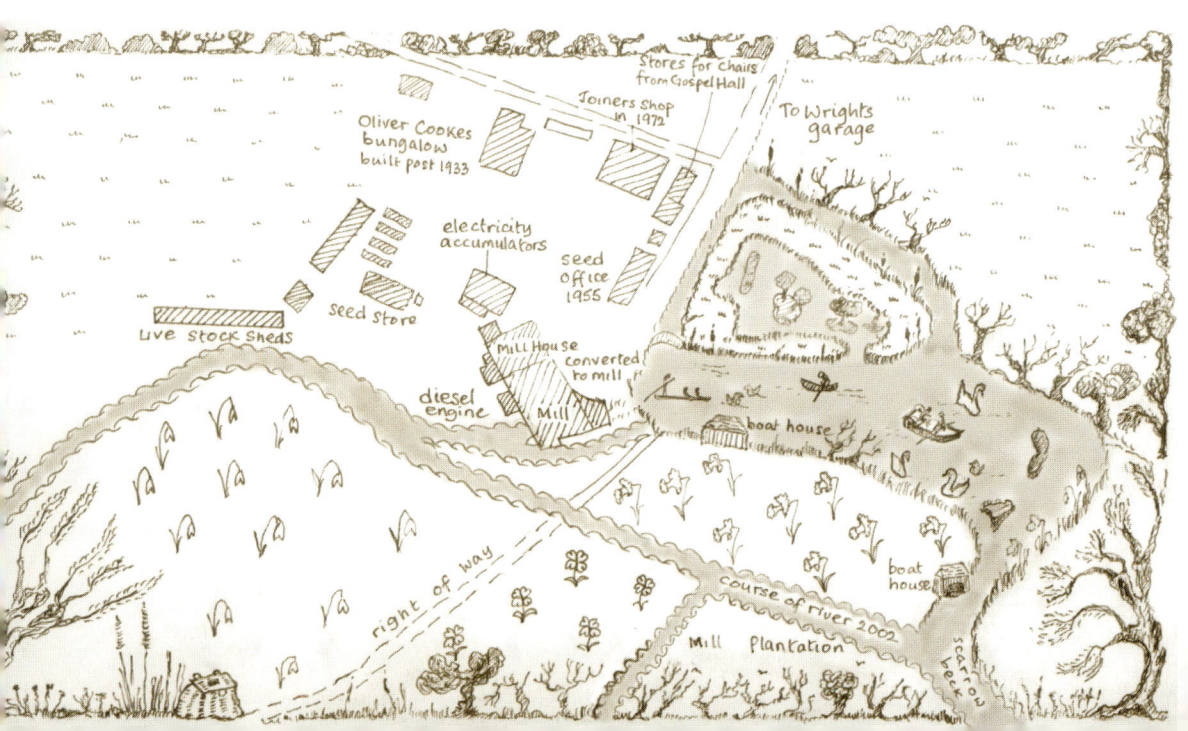

The parish border between Aldborough and Thurgarton is marked entirely by stream, and ninety years ago the whole area was very wet indeed.

The Great Flood
WI History

Aldborough and Thurgarton were much afflicted by the great flood in August, 1912. Every bridge on the boundary streams was carried away, and Aldborough was isolated except in the westerly direction until they were re-built. Goods were brought to one side of the stream and were slung across. Mr H. Underwood, a farmer living in Thurgarton was the last man to drive over the Thurgarton bridge by the old forge. The bridge gave way as he passed, and though he managed to get to the other side, his mare had to stay in the stream all the night. This mare gave birth to a foal the following spring which was called 'Floodtime'.

Floodtime in shafts. Fanny Suffling and Norah Underwood seated behind.

This flood made a big impact.

Ida Impson "1912, I think it was, August, we had the terrific storm and flood, and the man who lived in the farmhouse down at the corner in Thurgarton, had been riding somewhere with a horse and cart, and was then going home, over what had been the Thurgarton bridge; but he didn't know the bridge had been washed down, and that was all flood; he and his horse and cart all went into the meadow at the side which was then all flood - he managed to

The Underwood family of Manor Farm, Thurgarton

save himself and got out; but the mare that he was driving, actually, was then carrying a foal, and that was in the water all night; and when some of them went the next day to get this mare up on to her feet - well, in fact they thought she'd been washed out, she'd be dead, you see, drowned, but she wasn't, she was still alive. She'd had the foal she was carrying, so that was called Floodtime."

Albert Massingham "In 1912 we had the most dreadful floods, many bridges were washed away and the metal bridges constructed after the flooding went down are still in use. It is easy to pick out places that were badly flooded by these bridges ; they are all of the same design, some in Aldborough, Alby and other villages. I can clearly remember my brother Leonard helping to bale out our kitchen, never had seen so much rain before!! One mare that was being driven home by its owner that day was trapped in the flood water and this horse was in foal, it was rescued after 2 or 3 days, she had been held up by a fallen tree and her rescuers brought her out on a field gate. The mare was put up into a sling and she recovered, when the spring came she gave birth to a colt who was very aptly named "Flood" The owner of the mare was a Mr Underwood and the accident happened near the old Blacksmith Shop at Thurgarton."

The forge in its working days.

Temperance Villas, Thurgarton

The Massingham family were very involved with this particular flood, in one way or another! Here's a further anecdote as told to Rochelle, great-niece to both Albert and Ida, and written down by her.

On this particular day, their mother Edna had gone (over the river) into Thurgarton, to the end house in the row called Temperance villas, to help her own mother with her laundry. After the deluge, Edna realised she would not be able to get home through the floodwater, so decided to send a message with a wagoner, Thomas Reeder, who worked for Bone & Co. Thomas was prepared to try and get through and take his cart back up to the shop, so he was happy to take a message; but he was not prepared to take a person - he refused point-blank to give a ride to Albert Temple, a carpenter working at Hanworth, saying he was not prepared to risk anybody else's neck. Albert, however, was undaunted. At a given moment, and quite out of sight to Thomas at the reins, he climbed underneath the wagon, and came through the flood clinging to the axle.

winter wedding! We assume the [yo]ung man seated on the ground [to] be Edmund Gay, with his wife [D]aisy all in furs to his right.

Weddings
The Wedding of Margaret Gay of Aldborough Hall

On January 6, 1914, Margaret Gay married Revd Christopher Lilly at St Mary's, Aldborough. We include these brief entries from the diary of the bride's mother. The family held an 'At Home' the weekend before, to which all the neighbours on their visiting list were invited.

We had tea in both the dining-room and the morning-room. We had Quartette singers, a boy soloist and accompanyist on the piano - everyone seemed to enjoy the music very much. Part of the time the four men came into the hall to sing and their voices sounded very well there. The musicians had tea in the smoking-room, and Mr B. Lilly looked after them very kindly. The presents looked extremely pretty on the landing; Margaret's wedding-dress was on a stand, and the trousseau spread out in my bedroom, and the ladies all went in to look at them.

The wedding day itself.

We had hired two motors to come at 7. 30, they took Margaret, Bevil and the others to the Communion service at 8 o'clock. Margaret and I had breakfast afterwards by ourselves, and Edith looked after the rest. The two hired motors took our guests to church, one going on to Wickmere. Margaret and I went in our own motor. Edmund came to the church-yard gate to meet Margaret. The path was lined with villagers who followed into the church, making it quite full. The two Mr Lillys read the service and Bevil gave a very nice address. Margaret looked very sweet, and Chris very nice and earnest. The whole party came to this house afterwards, and we had wedding-cake and champagne in the drawing-room. Chris had a slight lunch in the library as he would not eat while driving, but we packed their luncheon-basket for them to take with them. They went off at 12.45, and arrived at Southwold at half past three.

The Underwood family farmed at Manor Farm, Thurgarton.

The wedding party consists of:
Bride - Norah Underwood
Groom - Jack Williamson
Others include: Eric Underwood, Mary Underwood, Herbert Underwood, Gerald Underwood, Irene Underwood, Doris Underwood; Bob Williamson, Bert Williamson, Vernon Twiddy

The First World War

Ida Impson's childhood memory of the day war on Germany was declared was still strong over 80 years later. Here she speaks of a family visit to Cromer, organised by her carrier father, Bob Massingham, in his cart.

Ida Impson "He could take that top off, so on August Bank Holiday, for quite a good many years he put seats round and would take loads of people to Cromer. One very vivid memory is the year when The World War broke out in 1914; I was eight; by some means we got the news that England had declared war on Germany - I never have known how we got the news; the only thing I could assume was, one horse and cart would come from Norwich GPO to various village post offices and deliver their stuff on the way, and perhaps the driver got the news by that means. Mother, my sister and me went with Dad that August Bank Holiday Monday to Cromer; father went to the Horse Inn and put the horses up with the man, and then we went on to the beach... After spending the afternoon there, we came back into Cromer to a street called West Street. People by the name of Amis kept a little tea-shop, where we

Soldiers in jovial mood.

The WI History gives the names of those who went off to fight, but who did not return.

Aldborough
Walter Leonard Bacon
Archibald Brett
Sydney Guy Davey
Edmund Gay
Herbert Lee
George Lewell
Oscar Martins
Sidney Martins
Frederick J.S. Spurrell
William Wilkin

Thurgarton
William Cooper
Frederick Green
Bertie Mallett
Russell Mallett
Bertie John Newstead
William Sizer

had tea - bread and butter and shrimps - which was a real treat. That year, 1914, when we came out from having tea, Dad said, "Well, I don't want to put the horses back in for a little while, we won't go down on the beach no more, we'll stand at the top and just have a look." And we went and stood on the top as he called it, and right in the distance, as far as we could see, there were ships going along; and my sister, who was two and half years older than me, said something which started me to cry; and then she cried too; and Dad said, "What's the matter with you two?" And we said, "Oh Dad, let's go home, look, Daddy, the Germans are now coming!" "Don't talk so silly, don't! The Germans? That's one of our trading ships going along there."

Up at the Hall, Edmund Gay heard the news, then immediately contacted local Army HQ in Aylsham, volunteering to serve. His mother, Mrs Gay, records the banal details of a decision which, tragically, would lead to his death, a year later, in the Suvla Bay landing.

August 4, 1914 We heard this morning that the English have declared war against Germany, so Edmund went into Aylsham and saw Mr Purdy, and offered to serve as a volunteer if he were wanted. Mr Purdy who is the Captain gave him a list of the things he would want, and said he would sent him a telegram if his offer was accepted. However, he received no telegram today.

August 14, 1914 Edmund had a telegram in the morning from Mr Purdy, telling him to join immediately. He motored to Norwich to see if he could get his uniform, but it will not be ready till 10 o'clock tomorrow, so he telegraphed back that he will go then.

August 15, 1914 Edmund went off in his car directly after breakfast...

29

This window on the south side of the sanctuary of St Mary's church, was given in memory of Edmund Gay, The dedication reads, 'To the glory of GOD and in loving memory of my husband EDMUND GAY Capt:1/5 Batt. Norfolk Regt. who was missing at Suvla Bay on 12th August 1915'.

Prisoners of War

As far as the village was concerned, war was noticed, first, through the absence of cherished men-folk, and next, by the arrival of prisoners accommodated in the Temperance Hall.

Cynthia Greene "I can remember the prisoners, German prisoners in the First War, they were in the Temperance Hall, (where we all signed the pledge, but we never kept it - yes, Leslie Kent did, you know, he wouldn't have a trifle if that had sherry in it.) Any rate, I can remember them marching the prisoners of war from the Temperance Hall to clean that mill dam out, I can see them going past as plain as punch. A whole lot of them, there were. I can remember them cleaning the rivers out around."

Albert Massingham "During the First World War some German prisoners were sent to clear the beck *(stream)* of weeds and the banks of old trees, this beck formed the boundary of my father's garden. My mother was out whilst the clearing work was in progress and when she returned she was furious to find that the prisoners had cut down one of her good apple trees but left an old willow standing!"

Ida corroborates her brother's story - but with a change of nationality!

Ida Impson "The Italian prisoners of war were in the Temperance Hall; they went out in days, going round various places, cleaning rivers out, ponds and so on, with soldiers on duty, of course. One of the prisoners was cook for them, and what had been a wash-house as you went up the yard to the back door of the house, that was his place for cooking. On Sundays they didn't go to work, and on Saturdays they worked till twelve or one, so they had the afternoon off. Funnily enough, when they did the stream that runs past where we were, we'd got a codling apple tree stood on the edge; and when they got doing that part of the river, or the beck as we called it then, they cut down what had been our codling apple-tree, which was the fault of the soldiers on duty with them, no doubt. Mother was rather put up about it…"

The WI History gives further information, before offering another variation on the nationality of those prisoners.

During the early part of the War, there was a Welsh Army unit stationed in Aldborough. The officers were quartered in Thurgarton Lodge, the men round the Green, a room in Kents' house being used as a club room.

German prisoners were quartered in Aldborough at the Temperance Hall. They were employed repairing the damage done to the streams by the Great Flood. They were mostly Austrians.

And evidence of the prisoners' work is provided through another source, the young Ron Dobbie, in his boyhood fishing days.

On page 24 (of the WI History) I note that German and Austrian prisoners were employed during World War I doing repairs to local bridges damaged by the 1912 flood (7 ½ inches in 24 hours) As a lad in the early and middle 1930s, I used to fish in the vicinity of the bridge at the bottom of Thwaite Hill, and I noticed several German names inscribed on the concrete abutments under the bridge. (I expect they are still there.)

Joe Hulls' Farewell

On August 18, 1923, Joseph Millington Hulls retired from his post as Head Teacher of Aldborough School. He wrote the following farewell message in the log book.

Joe Hulls This terminates my tenure of office as Head Teacher of Aldborough School, after thirty-eight and a half years of duty. I leave behind me a school in which obedience is deemed more than a duty, in which effort is considered of infinitely greater importance than result, and in which 'the best that I can' has been the ideal. Between the teachers and the children the relation is happier than in any school I have ever known. "In loco parentis" has always meant much more to all of us than the mere power of repression and punishment...

And that trust and confidence is not limited to the children, but is shared fully by the parents. Between myself and my staff the relations have been invariably of the happiest; no demand that I have made on them has ever been met otherwise than with perfect willingness and cheerfulness. So sure have I always been of their devotion to duty, that I have been enabled to allow them the most extended liberty in method and detail. I acknowledge in deep gratefulness all that they have done for me; they may all be trusted to the fullest extent to do all that their abilities permit, and to give real, honest, dependable service. The affection the children have for them is repaid by a love and devotion which is rarely equalled.

I part from both children and teachers with a poignant sense of sorrow; my chief consolation being that I shall still live near the school and in close association with it, and that in some measure I may still be able to assist. I wish my successor very wholeheartedly every success.

Before the Second World War
1920s - 1939

In this section we will take a detailed look at life in Aldborough and Thurgarton, paying particular attention to trades and businesses, many of them based on the Green. We combine the facts that have emerged in the course of our researches, with recollection, where available and appropriate. Some places and people prove more memorable than others!

Part One

The West Side of the Green	34
Traders	34
The School	44
The North Side of the Green	47
Traders	47
The Temperance Hall and Coffee Room Limited	49
Out and About	50
Aldborough Mill	50
Cuckoo Cycles	53
Rectory Farm	54
Doctor's Corner - Dr Eddy	56

Harry Varden
"Most of the people's needs were met by the village shops, and their money never left the village."

Many of the photos in this section are taken from postcards sold in the early years of the century.

The West side of the Green

Traders

*In its heyday there were at least 18 people working for **Bone & Co.** in Aldborough & Thurgarton.*

Elsie Davison "At fourteen I left school and went to work at Bone & Co in the drapery business; there was three of us in the drapery, and I was the apprentice; there was about 18 - 20 who worked there altogether - two people on the rounds all the while, with horses and carts, and then vans; Miss Lewell looked after their shop in Thurgarton."

Harry Varden "Of all the general stores, I best remember Bone & Co, for I spent six weeks with them, while I was waiting for Cooke's garage to be ready for business (1936). There is no way in which I can describe the smell, when you went through their doors. It was warm and on the whole quite a pleasant smell, a mixture of paraffin, sugar, vinegar, vegetables, clothes, calico, leather and many, many more things… That wasn't a thriving place, I suppose they wriggled along, wages weren't much, were they… that was riddled with rats - these old places were, weren't they? *(chuckles)* You went in some of those old outbuildings, there'd be such a rush, you'd hear these rats rushing out.. There was a lot of that… they used to cut the rat bites out of the cheese!"

Harry Varden "We went out on a horse and cart, an old covered cart, the front of the roof sort of came down to shelter you from the worst of the rain… *(chuckles)* the staff were just as fearful of the manager as we were of the school master… they were fearful of losing their job… (1936)"

Notes The drapery counter was to the right of the shop as you went in the front door; it ran nearly the whole length of the shop and had drawers under it. Three assistants served here. At the far end was the door out to the yard and the warehouses. All the walls to the shop had shelves full of stock. Immediately to the left of the door was the general office, then stretching to the back was the grocery counter, staffed by four assistants. The sweets, which were kept on shelves just beyond the doorway to the office, would be weighed out, then poured into a cone made out of paper by the assistant. Tobacco was available at the far end of the shop; this was weighed out by the half ounce, wrapped in a piece of paper, rolled over and over and then the ends were tucked in. On the back wall, directly behind the counter, were shelves with bags of sugar on them. These would be sold in blue bags of either one or two pounds. On Saturday nights the shop was open till 8 p.m. The staff weighed up the sugar, lard, butter and cheese ready for the following week.

Josh Lewell

*We have no first-hand recollections of Josh Lewell, the **Saddle and Collar maker**, although in its heyday before the First World War, the leather business was a vital part of the village economy. George Ewart Evans, social historian, writes in The Farm and the Village:*

The horseman was very particular about his harness and was as much concerned as the farmer to keep it in good order, making frequent visits to the saddler or harness-maker who had his shop in most of the larger villages.

However, the trade of harness-maker was already in decline in the twenties and thirties.

After the First World War, however, the tractor began slowly to erode the almost complete dominance of the horse; and although this process was slowed up considerably during the inter-war years by the depressed state of farming, the harness-maker had to adapt continually. (George Ewart Evans, Where Beards Wag All)

During these years some harness-makers found their skills still required in maintaining the leather and canvas of the self-binder or reaper-binder, which were still mostly drawn by horses at first. But the trade faced a bleak future.

Many blacksmiths and harness-makers - in the two crafts most closely affected - anticipated the farm horse's disappearance by closing their shops.

Josh Lewell shared the work available in the locality with Mr Sexton, whose shop was located in Thurgarton Street, and whose wife taught the piano. Mr Lewell sold his business to Mr Slaughter, who, however, quickly moved over the Green to become landlord of the Red Lion.

Gladys Miller/Dorothy Day "Mrs Readwin used to give us plum jam on bread; if Mother had given us that, we wouldn't have eaten it, now, would we! She used to say, "Mind the cobbles, mind the cobbles in the jam!" She didn't call them pips, she called them cobbles. Yes, and she used to give us a piece of cheese on some bread sometimes; and she said, "Now smell the cheese and eat the bread." And that's what we used to do! Her jam and bread was lovely."

The home of Mr & Mrs Readwin (now Manor Cottage)

Notes Mr Readwin worked as a baker, his wife plucked chickens, the room to the left of the front door was always full of feathers!

And many people kept poultry; Cyril Bacon remembers the poultry kept by the Chapman sisters.

Cyril Bacon "And Chapman had three daughters, they all had a poultry farm at the back of the Lion, where these girls worked, where they done their business, right down there behind the Lion, that was all meadow down there. That's where the girls earned their living."

We know of other poultry farms; one near the Watch Oak, run by Jack Williamson, and others up the Tanyard Road (now Thurgarton Road).

*Mr. William Spurgeon (senior) was the first **butcher**, followed by his son William (Billy).*

Notes The business was run by the Spurgeon family until 1947, when it was bought by Mr Leonard Massingham, son of Bob Massingham, the carrier. Leonard was already established as a butcher in the village. He'd started in the trade working for Harry Robins, a pork butcher whose premises were in the building (now called Penfold) just off the Green towards the garage. From there, Leonard set up on his own in 1928 in a garage on the forecourt of the Temperance Hall. He subsequently moved to a wooden shop in the garden of Olden Cottage. His daughter Joan Fisher remembers those times.

Joan Fisher "I do remember him delivering with pony and trap, as far as Briston and Melton Constable, and I used to go round with him, until we got the van."

Cyril Bacon remembers the shop at Penfold.

Cyril Bacon "There was a butcher there, a pork butcher, that's all he sold. Then Walter Pope came there, him and his wife, after that finished, and they used to go round with a little horse and trolley, selling carpets, second-hand clothes, all sorts of things... cotton reels, boot laces, the lot, you know..."

Fred Osborne outside the bakery

We continue along in a northerly direction. In Rose Cottage there lived Jack Williamson, the **tailor** who worked in a wooden shed on the north side of the Green.

Esmé Hurn (née Williamson) "We used to live in the cottage to the right of Spurgeon's the butcher's. There is an entrance up the side which allows access to the butcher's and in those days also to the bakery. They backed a delivery van up the yard one day and knocked our chimney down! We had no fire till it was rebuilt! The butchers used to slaughter the cattle and pigs in the yard sometimes, and the row was something terrible. It really used to upset my mother. There were also two outside closets in the yard and one day a bullock got out of the delivery lorry and rampaged round the yard, finally getting itself stuck in our closet! We used to share a water-pump in the yard with the Osbornes."

Next we come to **Old Bakery Cottage**, attached to the bake-house run by the Chapman family, who also worked from premises by the Red Lion. In 1934 the business was bought by Fred Osborne.

Cyril Bacon "That *(Old Bakery Cottage)* was Chapman's, now he had a baker's shop down the opposite side of the Green, joined on to the Lion. And he had 3 daughters, they all had a poultry farm at the back of the Lion, where these girls worked, right down there behind the Lion, that was all meadow down there. That's where the girls earned their living."

We move on to **Kents' Top Shop**.

Cyril Bacon "Wilfred Kent married a girl Day from across the Green, and she had the little shop there; it came out to the road.

They used to work that with the bottom shop, they sold the same in the Top Shop as they did in the bottom, sweets, tobacco, anything like that, you see. Why did they have two? Well they both had a big family, Day had a big family, Kent had a big family, that's why - as I say, you can go round the Green and they all had their little businesses, you see, and they all made a living."

Elsie Davison "Kents had a top shop there, what we call the Top Shop, where St Anne's Cottage is now, that was a lot of little cottages then; that was the drapery shop, for a start; and then that went into a little grocery one, with Mrs Chamberlain looking after it in the end, didn't she… but when that first opened a girl by the name of Doris Rowe had it as just a drapery shop."

John Brown's House used to be two dwellings, as the photograph shows. At one stage it housed the **bank** too! Before that it was the home of a **basket-maker**. John Brown based his **carpenter's business** in sheds behind the house. He was prominent in village affairs, acting as Parish Clerk for many years. He also took the role of Rate Collector and Registration Officer with Erpingham Rural District Council. He was by all accounts a shrewd man; records show that in 1926 he rejected the fee of £80 offered for the work, holding out for a higher sum. "With the extra running about entailed, he could not undertake the work at less than £100 a year." He got it!

Cynthia Greene "John Brown - he done everything in the village. If you had a broken pane of glass, he'd come and put it in, he was Clerk to the Parish Council for years, he was the Council! - he was a good carpenter, he did all sorts of jobs, anything you wanted done, I can see him with his apron tucked up. He had a son and a daughter, I was very friendly with her, but she went off the face of the earth, didn't she…"

John Brown & Rhoda

Notes WI History 1937
Some forty years ago a Mr Burwick lived in Mr John Brown's house. Behind the house, near Mr Brown's carpenter's shop, there were pits where he planted osier cuttings in the spring to grow ready for the winter. He used to take loads of skeps on his cart to North Walsham market.

39

Kelly Jarvis

Kelly Jarvis lived here.

As far as we know, Chesterfield House has never been home to a trade or business - but next door lived a man who played a key role in the daily life of the village.

Cyril Bacon "Kelly Jarvis, he was the **honey-cart man**; used to pull the tub round and empty all the toilets. And because that had iron wheels, he wanted them to give him some money to buy rubber tyres, and they wouldn't. That cost £12 if he'd a had that done, and they wouldn't do it. A lot of people was on the pull-the-chain job then, you know, he went to these Parish Council meetings, and he always asked them to give him this 12 quid to buy these rubber tyres, and they never would. They'd rather pay someone with a lorry to come and empty them, but they wouldn't give him that 12 quid. He pulled his cart, and when he came up the other side of the Green, his daughter used to hook on the front, trace-horse, yeah, his daughter! He was all right when he went downhill. He took it up Manor farmyard, up through there was a sand-hole where they used to dig sand out. Early on, he charged 3d. He used to go in the fish and chip shop across the Green, to Kents', and Leslie used to keep little bits of batter an' that, he used to keep him a bagful of that; and as soon as he see Kelly coming up the path, he ran down the path, and stuck that into his hand, wouldn't let him in the shop; if he did get in, everybody'd soon clear out! But he made enough money so he could buy a row of cottages down at Erpingham, three I think. But anyhow, he made a few shillings, he was always working, 'The Duke' they used to call him."

Cyril Bacon "The end cottage, there used to be an old gent who lived in there, his name was Hemblings; he wouldn't pay Kelly to empty his, and on a Saturday afternoon, when the cricket match was on, he used to get his pail out, put a sack over the top, and a rubber band round it, and he used to carry that straight across the Green, through the cricket match, they used to run in all directions! He went straight on down through to that lane besides Kents' shop, he had an allotment down there."

Anthony Day "George Jarvis went around with a tub on two wheels; we used to put a brick up his alleyway, so that used to spill over -

40

Georgie used to swear; once we took the pin out of his wheel, and the wheel come orf; once he tripped up in front of the Stone House here with a couple of pails he was then carrying down somewhere to bury up, he fell down and shot 'em all over the road; he then come into our stable as I was bedding the mare down, he come in there for a shovel to scoop it all up again - he'd been getting it up with his hands, I've never seen anything like it; what we used to do to that poor old fella, we'd play him up no end, we boys."

Harry Varden "They used to treat him very badly, old George Jarvis, he was butt of all the jokes…"

Anthony Day "There used to be an old gentleman, who lived in the cottage next to the Black Boys, in that row of cottages; they were my father's, he had them, there used to be an old man John Digle live in one of them; father had a four-wheel trolley with a hood on, him and another boy, they used to go to Cromer on a Tuesday with his horse and trolley, get a ton of coal, deliver it on the way home; they used to be gone all day! Then they went again on a Friday. They went to the coal-yard at Cromer, Cubitt and Walker it was, where Safeway now is… all us boys worked on the coal-yard."

The Black Boys

Cynthia Greene "And there was an old man called Long Tipple, he was about seven feet high - now do you remember Flood being in the Black Boys? I've seen him throw Long Tipple across the road many a time, drunk as a bone. There used to be a cockle stall on the end of that shelter - that went across the road with him, all the cockles, all the vinegar and everything else!"

Cyril Bacon "Spurgeon had his slaughterhouse up behind the Black Boys; they used to kill the sheep and pigs up there; the bullocks they used to kill up behind the butcher's shop, along the top of the Green. Where they built Fisher's house, that used to be all stakes with poles on, where they used to dry the skins out, the tannery."

Black Boys
A Morgan pub from 1896-1961

Landlords
1884-1901	John Suffling
1901-08	Alfred Jarvis
1908-16	William Flood
1916-25	Adelaide Flood
1925-30	Robert Williamson
1930-31	Arthur Andrews
1931-33	Robert Dent
1933-37	Alfred Lee & Edwin Shepherd
1937	Cecil Leverett
1937-38	Ernest Simmonds
1938-45	Alfred Lee

The Black Boys

Ruth Chapman is the little girl in the alley.
Rhoda Brown, Phyllis Hewitt and Muriel Colman are on the corner.
Cynthia is standing with her father and mother (Mr and Mrs Colman) in the shop doorway.
Garnett Brett, who worked in the cycle-shop, is the other man.

In 1919, Alfred Colman (known as Jimmy) bought the premises next to the Black Boys from a Mr Perkins. Earlier, he had taken an apprenticeship in **watchmaking**. *Cynthia Greene, his daughter, talks about his life in the early part of the century.*

Cynthia Greene "My dad used to go to Hanworth Hall, Gunton, Hanworth Rectory, Wolterton Hall, wind the clocks and keep them all in repair, look - that was a weekly thing. And I'll tell you another thing - before he was married, my father used to walk from down by the chapel to Cromer, by the main road, and come home via Sustead and Metton, have his lunch with brother in Cromer, walk all the way back, and clean grandfather clocks on the way. Now, weren't the days longer?"

Earlier, he had lived down on the East side of the Green, where he had been apprenticed to a Mr Hudson.

Cynthia Greene "Old Hudson died, and Mrs Hudson let Dad have his tools, and that's when he started up on his own, down there in that house by the chapel; his sister had had what they used to call a parlour, for a dressmaker's place; she got married, so Dad took over that room and did his watchmaking there, until he got married and moved house."

A comment from a customer!

Anthony Day "Jimmy Colman, he used to do watches and clocks, he used to keep them a couple of years before he done 'em! Tom Wilkin, he took his watch in, he used to go in to Jimmy Colman every morning and ask him the time - he soon done his watch, Jimmy say, 'Beggar me, I shan't put up with that!'"

The boys who tormented George Jarvis played games on Jimmy Colman too.

Anthony Day "There used to be a little hole in the bottom of the window, he used to sit there with his apron all tied round him, so if he dropped a wheel or anything it wouldn't go on the floor... we used to get a cigarette and puff smoke through that hole, and smoke him out!"

Cyril Bacon has this to say about the whole business.

Cyril Bacon "Jimmy Colman used to get Smith's watches from Smith's factory, a pocket watch they sold for 5 shillings; everybody had them, at that time o'day, he was a very clever man, I think, Jimmy Colman was - with his head, anyhow, that he was. He had his workshop facing the Black Boys, then you got the shop where they sold cigarettes and sweets, that sort of thing, bicycles tyres, what have you… He had his garage, Roy Brown was the man who done the bicycles up, and drove the taxi; then came the war, so Cynthia did the taxi work."

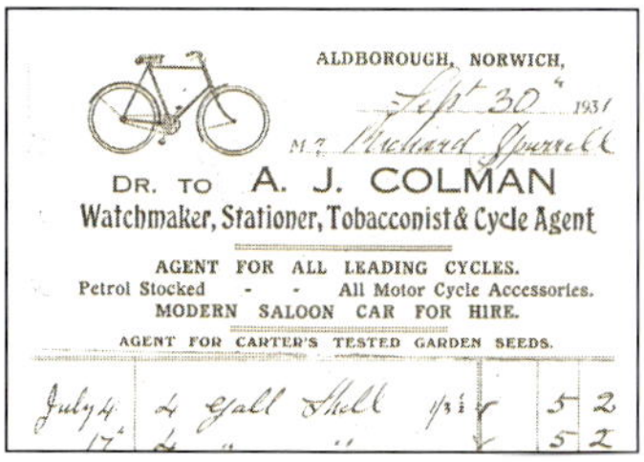

Jimmy Colman

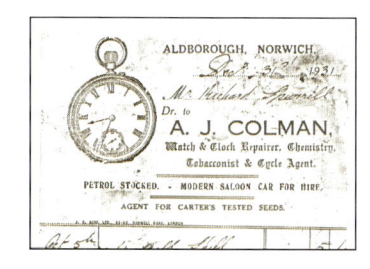

Examples of Colman billheads

Ford Touring Car for Hire

43

The School

In the introduction to the school in Section One, we had early mention of two particular individuals, Joe Hulls and Rose Earl. Mr Hulls retired from his post as Headmaster in 1923, after thirty-eight and a half years in the post! The first mention we have of Rose Earl is as a pupil in 1885, when she was commended by a Diocesan Inspector - as she was again in 1888 and 1890. By 1894 she had been taken on by Mr Hulls, as a pupil-teacher under his tutelage. In the school log he writes,

On Tuesday allowed Rose Earl to take first part of singing lesson and found it rather unsatisfactory. On Tuesday evening gave her a singing lesson in which, whether from nervousness or inability, she was unable to copy single notes.

A daunting experience for young Rose! However, progress was made and we read, in June 1898

Rose Earl is managing the infants well and I expect under her their intelligence developed in a much more satisfactory way than hitherto.

One of her pupils was Ida Impson.

Ida Impson "She was plump in body and friendly in manner, both in the class and outside of it. She was greatly loved by the children and the teachers. She was kind but firm - what she said she meant, and she stuck to what she said."

Rose Earl was, however, subject to lapses in health, as we saw earlier in the excerpts from the school log, and she was forced to have periods off, here and there, throughout her long career at the school. Matters came to a crisis in 1924, when, in addition to her teaching duties, she had to nurse her mother through a long period of illness. In the final weeks of her mother's life, she received stern rebukes from the Education Committee for both arriving late and having time off. She responded with this heartfelt plea.

After her mother's death, she continued working at the school, although her own health was clearly declining, and the first day of the summer term has this entry in the log, by Headmaster Mr W. J. Carter.

April 16, 1928 re-open school. I have to record with regret the serious illness of Miss Earl; she was found lying in the playground at 9.05 am as a result of a paralytic seizure. Medical aid was summoned and Miss Earl was conveyed to her home. Mr Hulls was present. Miss Howard is in charge of Infant room, 50 on roll.

And two days later the following was written within a black border.

April 18, 1928 With the deepest regret, I record the death of Miss Earl, which occurred early this morning. As pupil and teacher, she has been connected with this school for over forty years, and her tragic death is a great shock to us and to the whole district. She was the kindest-hearted person I have ever known.

April 20, 1928 I closed the school at midday, to allow teachers and children to attend the funeral of Miss Earl. Wreaths were sent by teachers, children and Old Scholars.

Immediately after Joe Hulls' retirement in 1923, Mr Wheeler was appointed. However, things clearly did not go very well; he was in the job for under two years, and the Norfolk Record Office holds this letter, written by a certain Mrs Davison, who was deeply upset by his treatment of her daughter.

```
                              Goose Lane,
                              Alby,
5th. Nov. 1924.               Aldborough.

Dear Sir,

    Mr. Davis, as you are the head of the Board of Education
I wish to ask you why so much caning is allowed in Alby School
by Mr. Wheeler.  My little girl was caned last week and her
hands were very sore for turning round, and also for putting
her pencils in her box.  She was caned again today.  I told her
to come home and she did so.  I intend keeping her at home
until something is done.  My little girl is quite afraid of Mr.
Wheeler which she never was of Mr. Hulls the late school-master.
We as parents are not allowed to mark our own children and why
should he.  Miss Earle one of the school teachers told me
Margaret was a good girl while in her class and quite sure did
not require the cane.  I am very sorry to see a man so fond of
a stick when he might look to his own.  I do not wish my
children to be rude to any one but I will not have them caned
in such manner.  I have been to see him but as he told me with
a grim (? grin) I have not a foot to stand on.  I am not sending
her to school to be ill-used.  We must all stand up for own.  One
woman went after him with brush and one boy knocked him over.  I
am not going to insult him so will you see to the matter.  Believe
me,
                    Yours respectfully,

                         "A.Davison"
```

However, Mr W. J. Carter was appointed in July 1925, and remained until his retirement in 1950, and the school flourished under his leadership.

February 22, 1926 The following report has been received from the Board of Education following the inspection of the 25 January, 1926.
This school was in an unsatisfactory condition when the present Head Master took charge in July, 1925. His efforts to effect an improvement have already borne fruit, especially in the upper classes, but much remains to be done before the school can be regarded as reaching a creditable state or level of efficiency.

Mr Carter clearly believed in community involvement.

July 7, 1926 Seventy children took part in an entertainment at Thurgarton Rectory this evening. Various school items, sketches, songs, a woodland play and country dances being given. Ten shillings was sent for the piano fund as a slight acknowledgement of the children's help towards parish funds.

The School Flower Show and Exhibition, inaugurated by Mr Carter, proved to be an annual event in the twenties and thirties, and were markedly successful throughout.

July 30th, 1926 The First School Flower Show and Exhibition held in the school was a great success. It was largely attended by parents and friends from all the parishes that the school serves. Classes for school garden produce, home produce, wild and garden flowers, table decorations, handwork, drawing, needlework, nature study, penmanship, composition and letter-writing were well-filled, and over two hundred prizes were awarded by the judges. Teas were served by the girls under the direction of Miss Preston; a Jumble stall was run by the Lower School teachers, and the numerous side-shows organised by the boys under Mr Sexton, school manager, contributed to the financial success.

Sport was not neglected.

August 6, 1925 The period 2.45 to 3.45 taken for purpose of introducing stoolball as an appropriate organised game for the girls. A match was played on the common between mixed senior teams, but a successful experiment was brought to a close at 3. 30 by a severe thunderstorm.

October 30, 1926 The Salhouse and Wroxham schoolboys visited for a Hospitals' Cup-tie. Opportunities for meeting boys from other schools are limited, and therefore it was pleasing to note the true sporting spirit that prevailed on this occasion. The visitors, in consequence of train delay, arrived with a depleted team; they suggested, however, that a start should be made following the half-hour allowed, by the home team, for the absentees to arrive. The home captain, winning the toss, decided to allow the eight opponents the benefit of the gale that was blowing. The decision probably cost Aldborough School the match, but it was an admirable illustration of the spirit of 'playing the game'.

Every opportunity was taken to increase resources.

November 1, 1926 Miss Newberry, the County Librarian, visited, with the travelling library van, to open a centre at the school of the County Library. After a brief explanation of the scheme, a small representative committee was elected, and 144 books were chosen.

Improvements made were duly noticed.

November 1, 1928 The following report has been received following a Board of Education inspection on July 31st.

"The Head Master, who was appointed in July 1925, is to be congratulated on the admirable results of his unremitting efforts to make this school a place of happy, progressive work and a centre of important educational and social activities of the villages. The curriculum is planned with great care; rightly, it contains large elements of practical work; varied and attractive forms of handwork for the Juniors and older girls, and gardening with older boys. Special mention should be made of the success in the instruction in gardening, and of the valuable effect it has had more particularly in stimulating increased interest in floriculture in the locality. The Annual Flower Show which includes also a display of the children's work in the various subjects of instruction, handwork, needlework, drawing and penmanship etc has been the means of securing the lively interest and wholehearted co-operation of the managers, parents and others in the work of the school. The attainments of the senior children are such to reflect great credit on the Head Master. The members of the staff are earnest and painstaking. In class 3, a very creditable standard is reached in all the subjects revealed. In the other three classes, much good work is being done, but some important aspects of training and teaching need more careful consideration.

North Side of the Green

Traders

Fernleigh House was home to the Spurgeon family for many years.

Anthony Day "Old Mrs Spurgeon used to sell the milk; they kept the cows down where Kents' shop is, down that loke; old Tom Fuller used to go down and milk the cows, walk right across the Green with two pails of milk, up to the old woman's house; then we went up there with a jug; she used to go to two pails to get it, she used to put a little water with it *(peals of laughter!)* - I don't know there's any truth in that, mind!"

*Next door was the **Post Office**, held by mother and daughter of the Chestney family. Then Miss Chestney came to marry Mr Chapman from neighbouring Chapman Row, and together they ran the Post Office from here until 1954. Ida Impson worked for the family after leaving school.*

Ida Impson "I was five when I went to Aldborough School and I finished at fourteen, when I went to work at the Post Office house, which was towards the top of the Green; I helped serve in the Post Office if necessary, and did work in the house, cleaning. Mr and Mrs Chestney lived there - he was the Postmaster - and there were two single daughters; the elder one, Nellie, was consumptive; she'd been in the sanatorium, but eventually she came back. Any telegrams which were received - we took telegrams then to various villages around - and I used to take them on my high bike."

The other recollection we have is to be found in a piece written by Joe Hulls' grandson in the Norfolk Fair magazine, in an article published in 1976. He remembers being sent on errands by his grand-father.

J.J. Maling However, even when my grandfather no longer ran the school, that was one of the few things in the district he didn't run. Even the Post Office came under his control to some extent. Many a time he sent me in there for stamps and postal orders, and had them chalked up on a slate hanging on the wall behind the counter. I think he was probably the only man who ever got tick in a Post Office.

In 1921 Bertie Day ordered a ton Ford van from America. It was covered with canvas at the back and cost £99. It was ordered through Cromer Garage and arrived in a wooden box. Afterwards, the box was extended and used as a garage for the van!

*The next commercial premises on the north side of the Green was the **General Stores** founded by Bertie Day in 1901. His five sons were recruited into the business, which developed to include a coal-yard, a bus-shed and general warehousing.*

Anthony Day "Father never used to work in the shop, only first thing in the morning at eight o'clock to fill up all the boxes he was going to take on his round, slide them in the old cart; and the horse used to stand there in front of the shop while he were loading up; he used to go off about ten o'clock; he come home at ten o'clock at night, have nothing to eat. He used to go to Felbrigg, round that way, and Roughton, Hanworth Common, White Post Road, all down there, Colby..."

Cyril Bacon "They were a big family, they all had a share in the business. They'd fetch coal from Aylsham station, go to bag it up; unless that was what they called steam coal - great old big lumps, which they used for the bakehouse and them sort of places; they used to take the scales and weights up there and fill it out of the truck. It was a big shop then - get anything you want, more or less. They had charabancs for the cricket matches, they'd have the board outside the shop for outings to Yarmouth Hippodrome, places like that."

In 1935, Bertie Day officially included his five sons in the business, which now traded under the name of B.G. Day and Sons Ltd.

Jack Williamson

*Next down the Green came a small wooden shed where Jack Williamson worked as **tailor**, making clothes for men, women and children. He also did alterations. (The bungalow named Perrotts now stands on this site.)*

Cyril Bacon "How Jack Williamson come about, he was in the army and he got wounded, and they sent him home, and they learned him to do tailoring, in the army; and they bought him that shop and business; he had irons up his leg. He used to sit on the board, you know how the tailors sit; he'd make suits, he'd alter your suit, do that for you, women's clothes."

Harry Varden "Jack Williamson had a tailor's shop, he was fixed up with that when he came home from the war, (1914-18), he had an iron on his legs, a calliper."

A.G. Davison & Son - In 1930, when Derrick Davison left school, his shoemaker father Alec built this brick shop for him as a development to the family business, carried on until then in a small room next to Kents' stores.

Elsie Davison "Now when Derrick came with him, he said, now if you want to stay with me, I'll build you a little place on that ground; so he built him the little shop; then during the war (1939-45), when Derrick went away, I came here to work with him. The new place was built when Derrick was fourteen."

Notes *The building had two rooms - a workshop and a shop. The former had one window facing the Green, and another at the side that looked up the Green. It was equipped with work benches and sewing- and finishing-machines for both making and repairing boots and shoes. It had an open fireplace and was lit by tilly-lamp. The second room was a salesroom with double windows and shelving for the stock. This was primarily for farm-workers, offering jackets, leggings, leather goods, Wellingtons and other types of footwear.*

Derrick Davison outside his shop

The Temperance Hall & Coffee Room Limited

The Temperance Hall was built in 1884 by a syndicate of wealthy local families strong in the Temperance movement. The aim was to provide a social facility for working people other than the public house; its full title made clear the nature of any beverage available - The Temperance Hall and Coffee Room Limited. The families involved included the Jarrolds, Gurneys, Barclays and Cookes.

Ida Impson The Hall was built by raising money through shares which were supposed to pay a dividend eventually, but they never did. They hoped to hold entertainments, but as they wouldn't allow gambling, dances, or any sort of wedding receptions, because drink would be sold, it never was a success. However, they used to have a coffee bar, where the young men could play draughts or dominoes.

This image is taken from a wood block owned by the Cooke family

49

It came to have a variety of uses, including that of base for Barclays Bank (open one day per week).

Anthony Day "They had a cinema in the Temperance Hall, when Charlie Chaplin was about; they had rollerskating in there. Metcalfs used to live in the house; the coffee room used to be the room between the Temperance Hall and the bank; used to go in the coffee room at night and stop in there till ten o'clock. Then Tom Cooke stored his grain and stuff in there, before the War. Cookery classes held in there before the war."

Cyril Bacon "When we was kids, Oliver Cooke and somebody else, they used to show slides, picture slides, we used to pay a penny or something to go to the pictures! That was a religious thing run by the Gospel Hall people. Tom Cooke finished up with it, and he used to store seeds."

Out and about
Aldborough Mill

On the death of his father in 1917, the twenty-year old Thomas Cooke was called back from war service to take over the running of the mill, a task to which he brought immense energy. In spite of a depressed rural economy, he saw many opportunities for business and pursued them vigorously. We read earlier of the non-conformist zeal in which he and brother Oliver were brought up, a zeal expressed both in his personal life and his business activities. At first his brother resisted the faith. Cynthia Greene has a typically astringent comment.

Cynthia Greene "He used to be the worst fellow that ever was born, Oliver Cooke did, and he died one of the best. And Tom always had the Bible under his arm, and he used to say, 'I shall win my brother over, I shall win my brother over.' And he did, too, didn't he?"

In their young days, the brothers displayed a spirit of invention in many areas.

Mary Carpenter (née Cooke) "They used to make fireworks as well, in the shed behind the mill… the two Cooke brothers always did a display on Aldborough Green. I've got a book of theirs with recipes on how to make fireworks…"

So Tom brought inventiveness and energy to the milling business. Expansion brought the end of the mill house as a family dwelling, and by 1930 it had been taken over as an extension to the mill premises. A diesel engine was brought in to augment and eventually replace water power, partly because water levels had dropped, partly to supply increased power to the various operations. Thomas Cooke was a great innovator of products, and over a period the business expanded to include the following activities.

- *Grinding corn for farmers - a continuation of the traditional role for millers.*

- *Seed corn prepared and dressed for sale to farmers.*

- *Animal feed manufacture - Tom Cooke developed on-site pig and poultry units to test his own formulas.*

- *Tested and sold seed of all types for both the agricultural and horticultural businesses.*

Here's an authoritative comment from someone who witnessed the exploits of the brothers Cooke over many decades.

Elsie Davison "They were terrific business people, Tom and Oliver Cooke, they were."

Oliver Cooke's Family

Oliver Cooke had a bungalow built for his family just over the way from the mill, and his four children, David, Jean, Mary and Jonathan grew up there. Jean has some tales to tell.

Jean Benzie For me as a child, the mill was not an attractive place - it represented rats and danger. The men that worked there had their trouser leg bottoms tied up with string to stop the rats running up their legs.

Here are some miscellaneous memories of time spent at the mill.

The original seed office was down by the side of the mill; Miss Millie Chapman was in charge of that. It was quaint with wonderful smells. Then the new offices were built, 3 in a row.

To a small child all that water in the millpond was very unfriendly, and the sluice was particularly frightening.

There was a very old punt that David used to use on the pond, and Dad before him; you had to manoeuvre this very long pole down into the mud and push yourself along.

I remember the pond being frozen many winters, and we could walk across to the three islands and pick the snowdrops. People came to skate on the ice, but there was a dangerous bit near the bridge that never froze over properly, where the water ran down and into the stream.

Uncle Tom kept pigs for a time, and ran a series of trials with pig-feed. There must have been 6 pigsties, and as a 3 yr old, I loved playing in with the pigs. Each pig was being fed differently. But one day, I decided to unbolt all the gates, and they all ran out and into the meadow. Poor Uncle Tom and his pig-man nearly went spare, but one of them hit on the idea of rattling their feeding troughs, and they all trotted back into the right sty!

On another occasion I rode bareback on a big old sow. She came straight for me, and I landed back to front on her, hanging on to her tail.

We used to climb down the bank of the stream just behind the mill and float pieces of wood, but if the men saw us, just for a bit of fun, they'd release the sluice and the water would come gushing out; we'd hastily scramble up the bank, I can tell you!

We had great times with the old sack trolley - big enough to hold 4 - 6 of us. We'd push it up to the top of the hill, jump in, and with David steering, we'd career round the back of the mill; David always managed to stop it just before it went over into the stream.

Cuckoo Cycles

Meanwhile, Oliver was also moving ahead. The young Cynthia Greene noticed his enthusiasms.

Cynthia Greene "And he was daft on motorbikes; this is true, he used to take the cart from the mill to Aylsham station, and he was so mad on motorbikes, he was reading a motorbike magazine all the way home and the old horse used to bring itself home. He never drove it home, there was nothing else on the road."

A self-taught mechanic, he quickly saw an opening in Aldborough for bike manufacture, sales and service. In the early twenties, he set up operations on Doctor's Corner, trading as Cuckoo Cycles. One of his employees, Harry Varden, recalls his skills.

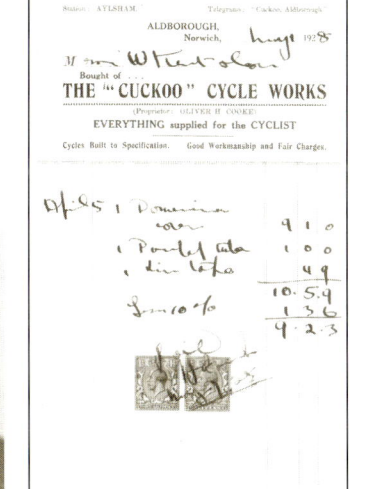

Harry Varden "He was very good at this, he'd spoke a wheel while he was talking to you. I don't think he learnt it from anybody, he just picked into it himself… "

With the growing number of cars, he was soon selling petrol.

Dorothy Day/Gladys Miller "I remember the cycle shop down near Doctor Eddy's, Oliver Cooke's old cycle shop; that's where he started. George Cook worked in there. I can remember when Father bought his Morris Oxford in 1933, I can remember fitting it up with petrol down there. Somebody else who used to work there, we used to call him Fiddy Lee, Eric Lee, and they used to call him Cookie's Oil-rags, *(peals of laughter)* he lived down Curtain Row."

The premises soon became too small, and he built a new garage for himself in 1936. Oliver's son David provides this summary of his father's work.

David Cooke "Before I was born, my dad was running a cycle shop down on what we now know as Doctor's Corner, the Cuckoo Cycle Works. He used to actually manufacture bicycles, because the police of this area always used to like to have one of his bicycles;

Standing in front of the garage are: Jack Knights, Harry Varden, Oliver Cooke, Cyril Howes, Gwen Goghlan.

well-built, heavy, very reliable; he used to buy the tube, then he would cut and manufacture his own bicycles; all the raw materials and wheels and what not, he would have all the spikes and he would make up the bicycles. Even today, there are some people around in Norfolk who have old Cuckoo bicycles, or remains of Cuckoo bicycles in their sheds! It's all gone, of course, absolutely nothing left; what little I remember of it, it was a sort of wooden building, shed-cum-garage; and the motor business developed from there. What is now A. Wright & Sons was what my father built and opened in 1936."

Rectory Farm

Oliver Cooke had his premises on land owned by the Filby family, who lived and farmed at Rectory Farm, on the corner of Calthorpe Road. Here we have an account (written in 1984) of thatching and threshing, farming practices which were still widespread in the thirties, but which disappeared with increasing mechanisation.

David Filby The hedges were always brushed (cut by hand) before the harvest and the 'brush' (trimmings) were used as the base of the stack. We always started off with a shock in the centre of the base of the stack to aerate the corn stack. Thatching was an art in itself and I still have a lot of the old tools at Aldborough. I remember father thatching and either Michael Allen or myself as the server (the man with the flail), and when father died then either Michael or I would thatch. We would start off with a long heap of good bunched wheat straw. This was then loosened and put on to another long heap, soaked with water and pulled out and straightened with fingers - in other words we 'gabbled' it. This was then put into the flail in layers about 2 inches or more deep by about 2 feet wide - about five or six layers in the flail at slightly different angles so the layers were kept separate. This was then tied up and carried up to the thatcher by the server. A large curved needle was used to sew the string into the straw. You cut and trimmed the thatch as you went, starting from the bottom of the eaves of the stack, tying each layer separately, and then working up to the top. A special thatching ladder was used.

When the stacks were thrashed, I remember that Wilfred Coleman used to bring the threshing machine and set it up with the buncher. Wilfred worked on the drum cutting the string on the sheaves. Noel Pope kept an eye on the general working of the machine as a whole as belts sometimes came off. Jackie Draper and George Jarvis were on the drum, Albert Finch usually on the straw stack. Wire netting was put around the whole area so that hundreds of rats and mice were caught and killed as they raced out of the stack. If workmen were not wearing spats they tied their trouser legs up with twine. I well remember a mouse running up inside my trouser leg and giving me a nasty nip before I realised why you tied your trouser bottoms!

Michael and I used to take the corn to the barn. Father would stack the corn. The drums then did a better job of cleaning the grain than the early combines. When we first used combines we often had to put metal rods down the centre of the sacks and leave them open to prevent the grain heating if weed heads had got through. When you finished threshing all the old calder and brushing and rodent bodies were burnt on the spot. The chaff was sacked up in large pulp bags and put in the chaff house to be fed to the cattle in the winter.

Here are some early memories of Rectory Farm from Daphne Nichols (née Filby).

Daphne Nichols In the large scullery at Aldborough was a large milk cooler next to the kitchen sink and pump. On the far wall where the door led into the garden was a large fireplace and a copper in the corner. Opposite the fireplace, the wooden work area with the milk separator on top.

The milk came in from the milking sheds and was put in the milk cooler, which was kept by the scullery sink. The churns were then filled and picked up every day. Our milk was brought home to Calthorpe House in a metal container which probably held a gallon. The milk for use by Nanny and Grandad Filby was separated from the cream, and butter was made from most of it for our use and to sell locally. Some was supplied to Bone and Co. When a lot of butter was made, a large wooden churn barrel type was used which I used to help turn, but when most of the dairy herd went a smaller glass one was used. Salt and a bit of colouring was added to the butter which was moulded and decorated with various fancy pats.

I used to collect the eggs from the chicken house in a huge wicker basket and was pecked by the chickens sitting on their eggs and more often than not given the added bonus of a flea or two.

Doctor's Corner - Dr Eddy

Dr Angwin Eddy was the village doctor during much of the lifetime of many people who have contributed to this book. He arrived as a twenty-six year old in 1929, worked in the villages throughout the following four decades and beyond, until his retirement in 1973. He moved into the house at Doctor's Corner very soon after his arrival and stayed there until 1981, when he moved into a bungalow on the north side of the Green. He was very active in all aspects of community life, and is well remembered both for a characteristic approach to his medical duties and his wider participations. He was captain of the cricket team in the thirties, he was a member of the Parish Council, treasurer and secretary of the PCC, churchwarden. He was very musical, and played the organ at St Mary's for a long period; he was an expert in photography. And he was easily recognisable through his choice of car - a VW Beetle! His first wife Phyllis wrote the WI History from which we have taken so much invaluable information; sadly, she died in 1946; in due course he married again; his second wife was called Margaret, a teacher of music; they had three sons. Let his patients speak!

Tony Barber "Dr Eddy you'd hear all kind of things about Dr Eddy; he was a very clever doctor; there were times when people said, 'Eddy doesn't care' and all the rest of it, but I always found him very helpful; he used to attend me in all kinds of situations on account of my asthma."

Rose Purdy "He was a very good doctor in the old-fashioned way, and he had no patience with malingerers; there was a tale of a man from a nearby village who went to the doctor and asked for some medicine. This was about the time it was first available free of charge. When Dr Eddy asked him what was wrong, and why he

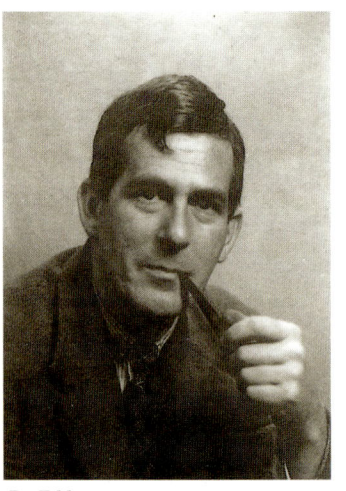

Dr Eddy

The WI Book gives the following list of doctors since 1780.

Dr Spurrell
Dr Woodcock
Dr Hacon
Dr Prangley
Dr Barton
Dr Findlater
Dr Heasman
Dr Higginson
Dr W. Spurrell
Dr M. C. Moxham
Dr J. A. Eddy

Cricket team list
G. Green (Sec.)
W. Carter
P. Carter
P. Chapman
T. Pike
E. Attew
W. Spurgeon
E. Howard (umpire)
D. Gee
J. Shales
Dr Eddy (Capt.)
G. Wolstenholme
R. Howard
L. Kent (Vice Capt.)

thought he needed medication, he said, 'If it's free, I'm entitled to my share.' 'If you feel like that, I'll give you some,' said the doctor. When the man got outside he took a good swig from the bottle… he took a long while getting home, he had to jump over the hedge every few minutes. He wasn't in such a hurry to get medicine after that!"

Donald Colman "He didn't need to send you to hospital to be X-rayed, he could X-ray you by looking at you! He was a very clever man."

Billy Hammond "He was a no-nonsense doctor, often short with his patients."

Daphne Nichols "When I was four, I kicked him in the shins because he hurt as he was stitching my head here, so he turned me up and smacked my backside."

Billy Hammond "I remember my father squaring him up; there was a terrible crash by Thurgarton police house, involving one of Osborne's little green motors. My father was up that way, and he quickly went and got the doctor, who wasn't too concerned… my father told him to go and give the woman the attention she needed; my father was a strong man, and the doctor went."

Donald Colman "There was no heating in the waiting-room, it was like an ice-house, and the draught came through the door…"

Daphne Nichols "Before the National Health you didn't go to the doctor's more than you could help; you had to be really bad, because you had to pay 2/- or something… I can remember being sent home from Aldborough School with spots all over me, and Mr Carter told me to go straight to the doctor; and I did, and he said, 'Tell your mother she owes me 2 shillings.'"

David Cooke "He certainly didn't like any patient who would go to him and then try and tell him what was wrong, and what treatment he ought to give… that would be the quickest way to do a U-turn out again."

As for his wider participations…

Ruth Bayes "He was very friendly with Mr Ketton-Cremer who lived at Felbrigg, and actually took some of the photographs that are in his books."

Tony Barber "But he was a lad, he used to go round the villages, you know, always carried a shotgun in the car; when, as a boy, I was out with Father in the car, he'd say, 'Look out, Eddy's ahead of us!' and there would be Dr Eddy out of the car, with his shotgun over the top, he didn't bother with the pheasants that were flying, he would take them on the ground; I don't think Mr Burrell Hammond liked it, he'd turn up at harvest, when there were rabbits, with his shot-gun, he didn't turn him away, but he didn't like it, he would blow the rabbits to bits, he could never shoot, he was a terrible shot."

Billy Hammond "When Dr Eddy was playing the organ, he used to like the curtain drawn one side, rather than completely on the rail, so that he could look round and see a certain lady during the service…"

octor's House

Christopher Eddy died at the age of eighteen in January, 1972

Tony Barber "And he went to see a girl-friend on a regular basis, everyone took it as being normal…"

He suffered a great personal tragedy.

Tony Barber "One of his sons died as a youngster, he ran upstairs, a blood vessel broke in his brain, killed him outright. The doctor was terribly shocked by that."

But he did know his Bible.

Freda Parker (née Osborne) Dad bought The Old School Cottages for some of the workers to live in, as well as some land across the road. Dr Eddy rented some of this land, but eventually Dad had to give the doctor notice. I presume he needed that plot for one of his men. Anyway the doctor was furious, and came down to our house to argue his case for keeping the land. As he left the house, without the result he'd hoped for, his parting quip was, "Now I know why Pharaoh hung the baker!"

Details of Old School Cottages when they were sold off in 1947

LOT 1.
AN ATTRACTIVE
SMALL HOLDING
KNOWN AS
THE OLD SCHOOL HOUSE
COMPRISING

A charming Old World Country Cottage facing South, well built of Red Brick with Tiled Roof.

Containing: Entrance Porch, Dining Room with fireplace and power plug. A very pleasant Drawing Room with Bay Windows and Tiled Stove, Tiled Entrance Hall with cupboard under the stairs. Leanto cladded shed used as a Kitchen with sink connected to soft water tank. Wood and Corrugated Iron Wash House with copper and furnace. Coal House, Store Shed and Closet.

2 well lighted Bedrooms, one with tiled fireplace.

A large Building with cladded walls and boarded floor formerly used as a school. Tastefully laid out front Garden. Small enclosed back Garden. Pump and Well of Water. Electric supply connected.

Small enclosed Piece of Arable Land extending to about 1 Acre (more or less).

As in the occupation of the Vendor who gives

VACANT POSSESSION ON COMPLETION OF THE PURCHASE.

TOGETHER WITH

TWO SUBSTANTIALLY BUILT

RED BRICK AND TILE COTTAGES

each containing Sitting Room, Kitchen and 3 Bedrooms. Closets and Brick and Tile Outhouses with productive Gardens planted with fruit trees. Good Well of Water with Pump. As in the respective occupations of Messrs. Greene and Lambert at Rentals amounting to £19 16s. 1d. per annum. Owner paying Rates. The wooden sheds on the Gardens are the property of the tenants.

Also a Small Enclosure of Garden Ground planted with fruit trees as let to Dr. J. A. Eddy at an annual Rental of 10/-.

TENURE FREEHOLD.   OUTGOINGS

And Freda has the last word.

Freda Parker Mum always respected Dr Eddy. As a child, I frequently had asthma and Mum told me that on one occasion, when I had a bad attack, the Doctor came out to me in the middle of the night with an overcoat over his pyjamas. Of course, this was in the days and (nights) before inhalers. Almost always, when the doctor visited our house, he would play a tune on our piano, either when he came or before he left.

Before the Second World War
1920s - 1939

Part Two

The East Side of the Green	60
Traders	60
The Reading Room	63
Traders	64
The Bowling Green	66
The Church Room	67
Places of Worship	67
St Mary's Church, Aldborough	67
The Primitive Methodist Chapel	69
All Saints' Church, Thurgarton	69
Thurgarton Talk	70
Bone & Co., Thurgarton	70
Thurgarton Bull	70
Thurgarton Street	71
The Chapman Family of Low Farm	73
Aldborough & Thurgarton WI	74
Village Talk	76
The School	78
Mattie	80

Harry Varden
"In my early days, on the lower part of the Green there was quite a large pond, with many geese, which were very aggressive to young children, if you went too near."

Blacksmith shop

East Side of the Green

Right down in the corner of the Green, opposite the Temperance Hall, stood the forge run by Arnold Pentney. The iron rings where horses were tethered are still set in the brickwork. The Chapman girls remember.

Dorothy Day/Gladys Miller "Old Pentney the *blacksmith* lived at Calthorpe, where he had an orchard. He used to bring us an apple, which he'd get out of his dirty old jacket, with his filthy old hands; we used to eat them and thought they were lovely! We've eaten our peck of muck or whatever you should do before you die - probably put years on to me!"

Cynthia Greene "Pentney's blacksmith's, we used to watch him shoe the horses, and we used to watch him do the wheel round the hole in the ground, they used to steam, didn't they?"

Harry Varden "The best place to find anything out was Arnold Pentney's blacksmith shop, all the news came from there, old Jonah Rowse the roadman, he'd be in there half his time… they were called lengthmen in those days, they had their length, so much road, he'd mend all the pot-holes and trim the corners where weeds came up… and he'd get on to farmers about carting the mud on to the roads - no doubt they paid him so much to keep quiet…"

Next door was one of the three bakeries on the Green.

Harry Varden "George High the *baker* - I particularly remember him, he would be round with his Hot Cross Buns about 7 a.m. on Good Friday, with the buns they'd been up all night baking; this was a one-off thing… they called his son Wind-Up, because he used to sell his Wind-Up self-raising flour… when he went to school, they said, 'Here come Wind-Up!' They didn't have much equipment, I mean Health & Safety people would have a fit, full of cobwebs and flour, like a snow-storm in the winter!"

Harry Varden adds a memory of a long-lost skill with spittle.

Harry Varden "Fred Jarvis (old George's brother, I believe) used to live down High's Loke, he used to chew baccy. Well, you know how they sort of nipped the face together, when they chewed tobacco… and then this jet comes… I mean, if you haven't seen it, you can hardly describe it really… but people said he could hit a fly on a wall at ten yards!"

*Fred lived in the hut that had been the workplace of Mr Martin, **whip-maker**, mentioned in the WI History, in its general survey of the Village Industries based in Aldborough.*

Glove-making This died out in the late 19th century. It is mentioned in the records of the 14th century. The industry was carried on at the end of the loke past Mr High's bakery, and there were open pits used in tanning leather there.

Tanning "There were two tanneries in Aldborough, after one of which Tanyard Road is named. Little is known of this. The other belonged to Mr Miller (about whose spiritualism some curious stories survive) about 1900. He used to purchase dead horses for conversion into leather. His tannery was on the east side of the Green."

View of Pentney's Blacksmith Shop and High's Bakery at the bottom of the Green, also showing the drainage system at that date.

Whip-making was carried on by Mr Martins in a shed near Mr High's bakery *(now Victoria Cottage)* until his death in 1930.

*Next door to High's **bakery** is the building, now Fox Cottage, which used to be the Methodist chapel. It retains the original door. Mr Catchpole, **bricklayer** and **chimneysweep** lived here in 1937. Robert Bacon, **wheelwright**, lived in the next house, Greenside, followed in 1933 by William Mayes, **carpenter**, who likewise had his workshop here. Among other things, he made coffins for Mr Kent, Funeral Director.*

*The leather trade (in the form of a **currier**'s business) is thought to have been based in these houses. A very watery spot!*

Baldwin's Shop

*The building now known as Kent's Place used to be a shop. Jimmy Colman started out as **watchmaker** here, before moving up the Green. Jimmy Colman's two sisters, Tilly and Hilda, continued to work on the premises; Tilly (Newstead) was a **dressmaker**, while Hilda opened it as a shop selling sweets and stationery. After her death in 1923, Tilly's daughter Olive took over the business while her husband Herbert Baldwin worked as **butcher/slaughterman** for the Spurgeons. Olive expanded the range of goods on offer to include food, **pharmacy** and fancy goods. In the evenings and weekends, Herbert worked as **barber**, in a curtained-off area at the back of the shop. During the war he drove a lorry for Oliver Cooke. The shop closed in 1969, and Mr Leslie Kent bought the block.*

Esmé Hurn "I can remember when Herbert Baldwin the chemist hurt his leg and was laid up. He made some tubular contraption with a mirror in the end and this was put out of the upstairs window so he could see who was in the road and talk to them! We used to stop off for sweets and father gave us a halfpenny, and said, 'There's a farthing for today and one for tomorrow.'"

The Reading Room

The Reading Room

On the right of the photo on page 61 stands a building which is no longer there, although it appears familiar - because it moved a few hundred yards down the Chapel Road! In the twenties and thirties it was the Reading Room, used for various purposes, one of them an advice centre, manned by Joe Hulls.

Elsie Davison "He used it for people for any help they wanted, he used to talk to them, anybody used to go to him for advice or anything like that; I was only five, but I do remember my people talking about him."

Cyril Bacon "That was Old Joe Hulls' - he had his office in there - he used to let the lads and girls and whoever wanted to go, that was a Reading Room, you see, you could go and have a game of cards, or anything like that. "

It was available for rent too.

Dorothy Day/Gladys Miller "There was a building in the yard. Mr Moore, who was a chemist, lived at Cawston, came by train to Aylsham, then walked from Aylsham to Aldborough; he was a little short man with a bowler hat he used to wear and a little black bag, I can see him now. Mother used to say, "Go down to Mr Moore's and get some pink pills." They were some little pink pills; we used to think they were marvellous pills, they did us no end of good! That little wooden place is at Thurgarton now, old Miss Carver used to live there during the war."

Audrey Day "He used to come every Thursday, with his pills and potions, what anyone wanted; Anthony said, if we had a cough, Mother used to send us over there for Fox's cough mixture!"

William Kent ran Kents General Supply Stores until his death in 1932. His sons Leslie and Wilfred took over the business, adding a new shop front in 1935. Leslie and his wife Mildred worked in the premises on the east side of the Green, Wilfred and his wife Ena running Kents' Top Shop opposite them.

Elsie Davison "Kents' was a *General Stores*, he had everything, coal and coaches and everything, funeral directors, he had a *fish and chip shop* down the back there, one of those little old houses."

Audrey Day "And they used to have fish and chips at Kents', where the old garage is, Saturday nights. That stopped because of the war, because of the lights, used to get a good old bag of chips for tuppence."

William Kent in the doorway of his shop, many of his wares on display.

64

The cobbler's shop

Inside Kents' General Stores.

William Kent let out one small room to Alec Davison, shoemaker.
Dorothy Day/Gladys Miller "Old Alec Davison worked in that little tiny shop on the end of Kents'; we used to sit there and watch him; he'd get a handful of nails out of an old tin, put them in his mouth... I used to go there dinner-times, and if there was anybody sitting on the end seat where I used to go and sit, I used to be so disgusted; I used to call him Davo, and I used to say to him, "Ooh..." and he'd say to them, "Do you mind, she'd like to sit there, she ain't got long to stop." - 'cos I used to go and watch him every dinner. We used to watch him sewing shoes; he'd make a pair of boots for these old farm labourers, they'd last a lifetime."
Brian Kent "He had a little room, the floor used to be smothered with tacks and studs and things."

Harry Varden "I've sat and watched him doing that, that's very interesting; they used to have what they call wax-bond ends, that was on a hog-bristle; he'd make this hole with an awl, then put this hog-bristle through, then he'd pull them tight, you know, they kept crossing... to put the sole to the welt... I love seeing people work when they're good at their job."

WI History (1937) "Next a group of three houses built in the late 17th century. The first was until recently a *bakery* owned by Mr P Chapman, and is now occupied by his widow. The other two became the *Red Lion Inn* in the last century."

The Chapman bakery was situated in the single-storey extension jutting out towards the Green, comprising the bakehouse and later, the shop. The family lived behind. The bakery business used to operate on both sides of the Green.

Cynthia Greene "Now Mrs Chapman was always walking from one side of the Green to the other, with loaves - they only had one room in that house, you know."

Bowling Green

Cyril Bacon "The bowling green, that was theirs *(the Red Lion's)*, I used to go with my father to cut it on Saturday afternoon, he'd push at the back and I'd pull at the front, sometimes twice a week. Those old men wouldn't half create if they come along there and that hadn't been cut properly...Huh! Mustn't cut it up and down the way they played, you'd cut across it, so you've got all them scooty bits to run in at the finish, you know. Eventually they got a motor mower; I got fed up with that, I said to my father, 'You'll have to tell 'em to get somebody else to pull it!' We cut the hedges all round, and the banks, you know."

Landlords of the Red Lion 1879 - 1959

1879 - 1909 *George Wilkin*
1909 - 1915 *Thomas Tudman*
1915 - 1923 *Thomas Kifford*
1923 - 1927 *Robert Bowditch*
1927 - 1931 *Charles Smith*
1931 - 1939 *Jack Harmer*
1939 - 1959 *Mr & Mrs Slaughter*

Up to 1967 the Cricket team used the Red Lion as its base and dressing-room.

The bowling green was in the garden to the south of The Red Lion.

The Church Room

Our tour of the Green brings us to the last building in existence at that time, the Church Room. It was enlarged in 1933.

WI History The Women's Institute meets here, and it is a most useful room for concerts, whist drives and meetings of all kinds. It has a well-equipped stage and dressing-rooms, but unfortunately is not financially self-supporting.

Cyril Bacon "The Lilly family started it, and they had the running of it; Margaret Lilly, the parson's wife, nice woman, she was one of the Gays from across the meadow there at Wickmere. Very big woman - he was big, too - but I know she was a good woman. Going along the Green, that was Chapman's poultry farm; there was a gateway off the Green into their poultry farm, and that went a long way down the back way."

Donald Colman "There's one interesting thing she was involved with years ago, it just show how things change, every Saturday afternoon we had what they called a King's Messenger class in the Church Room. It was run by Mrs Lilly and her sister-in-law Mrs Gay; we used to make all sorts of things - baskets, mats, we used to knit, to sew, we never thought of going to football matches on a Saturday afternoon, we always used to go to the Church Room. That was all the time, from the time I started school till the time I left school, 1927-36; we then had a sale once a year up at the Rectory, all the proceeds went to some children in Africa; we had a Sunday School class, and it was those children who went… There was also a Church Guild, we went up the Hall once a week, play games, have a General Knowledge quiz, and a party once a year."

Places of worship

St Mary's Church, Aldborough

Christopher Lilly was Aldborough's Rector, from 1914 until 1946.

Well before his induction early in 1914, Mr Lilly had already been engaged to Margaret Gay of Aldborough Hall, and was actively searching for a parish in Norfolk. Now it so happened that St. Mary's incumbent, the Reverend G.W. Borlase, announced on 5 October 1913 that he was going to Market Rasen, and Christopher Lilly, intent on a living in Norfolk, was admirably placed to take over. He married Margaret Gay on January 6 1914, gaining special permission from the Bishop to live in the Hall, and not the Rectory. In 1916, he became, in addition, chaplain at Kelling Sanatorium.

There had always been a rumour of an underground tunnel to the church, but this was confounded on 2 Aug 1923, when Mr Lilly 'superintended the opening of the vault' and no secret passage was found.

He was a busy man!

Daphne Nichols "Services on Sunday were an early Communion

Notes on building and furnishings of St Mary's

1906 West window replaced
Bell turret given in memory of *James Gay*

1910 Organ given in memory of *Edward Gay*

1914 Oak lectern given by the Rector and Mrs Lilly

1920 Consecration of extension of churchyard

1920 Dedication of War Memorial tablet

Memorials to men who fell in the Great War

Oak choir stalls

Pulpit

Oak altar top

Dedication of Sidney Guy Davey window

at eight o'clock, nine thirty would be Sunday School, eleven o'clock Matins; two thirty afternoon Sunday school, six thirty Evensong. Dr Eddy played the organ at services, Miss Johnson for Sunday School. Miss Johnson lived either the second or third cottage past the thatched house. Mr Readwin pumped the organ; he lived in the detached house before the butchers. Mr Wells was churchwarden and gravedigger."

An annual event was the Egg and Flower service, held on Low Sunday; on one occasion, 394 eggs were counted!

Daphne Nichols "We would spend hours on the Saturday morning picking primroses to decorate the church. We took eggs which were distributed to the hospitals and homes."

Family income was very low throughout this period, reflecting the poverty widespread in the community. For example, the churchyard holds very few gravestones from the thirties.

A highlight of the year were the 'treats' held up at Aldborough Hall by the Rector and Mrs Lilly for the Sunday School. These were held for children from all denominations.

Daphne Nichols "The Revd Lilly lived at Aldborough Hall, where we had our Sunday School outing every summer, and shared it with children from a home at Gresham. We had a lovely tea, always with raspberries, in this long room, on the side of the house. We had sports in the park, where we competed against the home; big boat-swings were hung in the oak trees and we also had games on the lawn - a fantastic day out. I suppose we walked, I don't remember anyone taking us - it was quite a long walk to Aldborough Hall. Denys and Christopher Lilly and sometimes Geoffrey were there with their parents helping to make the day great for us all. We were given medals at Sunday School for attendance, gold, silver and bronze; we would go when we didn't feel well just to get our medals at the end of the year."

Billy Hammond remembers going to church as a small boy in the thirties for another reason.

Billy "I used to make air for the organ, I quite often did that; my mother didn't miss a service at all, but father wasn't very regular; however, I had a spell of fainting, and that was due to the smell of flowers; this would be in the spring or summertime. My father used to get hold of me and take me outside, sometimes I came back; but he got fed up with me. Once - and this was the last time this really happened - he put me outside and chucked me down and went back into church. Well, he put me right down on an ants' nest; I must have had a heavy faint that time, I was bitten all over with ants; the doctor was playing the organ, he ordered me home straight away - I can picture all this in the house now - but I laid on tons of newspaper, and the doctor came and put ointment over me; I was on newspaper because that would have spoilt all the sheets.

And because I was a nuisance in always fainting, I went for quite a spell without attending church... I must have blown that organ when I was six years old, in 1932."

The Primitive Methodist Chapel

The only story to surface is about Carol-singing at Christmas.

Ida Impson "We were all members of the Primitive Methodist Chapel - about a dozen of us - and we'd go carol-singing on Christmas Eve, but we wouldn't start until nine o'clock at night, so we'd be singing all night. We used to start by walking down to Aldborough Hall; when we came away from the Hall, the next place was the Rectory, where a man called Mr Guy Davey lived with his French wife.

When we went there the second year, she came out with a big white bag in her hand; Gerald Underwood had gone forward to collect the money, and she said to him, "Just to help you on your peregrinations".

Gerald said, "Thank'ee, ma'am".

Of course, when we set off again, and got out of their front drive on to the road, we all got round Gerald, and asked him, "What we got in that white bag, Gerald, what's in it?" Well, there were some mince pies and little cakes of some kind. Gerald answered, "Peregrinations, or somethin' - what she say?"

Now Ernest, my young man - we weren't married then - said, "Just to help us on our peregrinations."

"Peregrinations," Gerald said, "what the deuce do that mean?"

And Ernest said, "On our travels." I don't know how he come to know what it mean. Then of course we all dived into it and had something to eat!"

All Saints Church, Thurgarton

Thurgarton church is a handsome thatched church, that served a small population, most of whom lived some distance away.

For much of the twentieth century, a tenacious congregation strove to maintain All Saints as a place of worship, against a background of low income and a large and leaky roof. In June, 1922, a major fund-raising event was held in Wolterton Park, at which police were on duty at 3 shillings per hour; this may well have been to raise money for the War Memorial, designed and created by Mr Robertson, a skilled wood-carver who lived in the parish. The church was crowded for its unveiling on Palm Sunday, 1924. However, costs were such that two years later, the balance on the annual accounts was recorded as 3 farthings! A possible solution to this precarious situation was a draft scheme to unite the parishes of Thurgarton and Sustead, but this was firmly rejected. Meanwhile, the roof continued to deteriorate.

Ladies and buckets on the Chapel steps!

Thurgarton Talk
Bone & Co.

In the early years of the century, Bone & Co found it made commercial sense to open a small branch of their store in Thurgarton. Most of the goods available in the main shop on the Green were also sold 'over the stream' in the neighbouring parish, in what had been the front room of a house built in 1845. Miss Lewell ran the shop, before Elsie Davison - Elsie Hunn at the time!

Elsie Davison in the door of her shop!

Thurgarton Bull

The Bull Inn dates back well into the nineteenth century. We pick up its story in 1933, when Benjamin Farrow and his wife Nellie took over as landlords. They ran the pub for nearly a quarter of the century - it closed finally in 1957. The premises were sold on to Julie Pryor and Ray Ferrier, who carried out a very full research into its former days. They enjoyed long conversations with Nellie after Ben's death, and have provided extensive information, from which the following is a small selection.

The Bull Inn in the thirties

Pub landlords at this time often needed other sources of income; Ben Farrow was a skilled carpenter and wheelwright.

The inn had the barn for Ben's workshop and two sets of stables on to the yard, the upper and lower. Before Ben and Nellie's time, the lower stable had been used to smoke herring and the beams were all blackened. The backyard was cobbled, with six-foot gates that could be locked at night - but with a small courtesy door. The front yard was also cobbled, with ringles in the walls to tie up horses. The barn was used for the brew drays overnight - there used to be a delivery run from Norwich each week.

Running the Inn

There was no bar; beer was kept and served in the cellar (half below ground level), and brought to customers on trays - tiring work! The

Ben & Nellie Farrow

List of landlords

1904 John William Tice - Victualler
1912 Frederick Mallett
1916 Frederick Mallett and
 Edward Harrison - Victuallers
1922 Edward Harrison - Victualler
1933 Benjamin Farrow
1957 The Bull closes

kegs were laid on oak trestles, which ran along the cellar wall which adjoined the Long Room. There were oak settles around the walls of the Inn kitchen, and a 'spinner' in the ceiling for gambling. This room clearly shows the marks of many years of use by hobnail boots, and Nellie described many nights when the men would step-dance in this room. There was a big open fire where the beer was mulled with a poker to make 'poker beer'. A Ladies Room began over the war years, and the Long Room is where events and dances were held, and where club meetings took place - including the 'club' that people paid into weekly and drew on in time of sickness.

The Barn

This was sometimes used as a skittle alley, but it was mainly Ben's workshop, where he made farm-carts and trailers; sometimes with an audience of school-children, permitted to watch and chatter, on the condition they did not touch his tools. He went to market in Holt each week by pony and trap, and continued horse-dealing while there was still demand for horses on the land. Nellie decribed feeding and bringing them back into condition, helping Ben pour elixir down their throats, guaranteed to cure a broken-winded horse - at least for a short time! We found the hag-stone which was kept in the stable to protect the horses against witchcraft.

The Bull

John Neill tells an amusing incident of pub horseplay (literally!)

John Neill "There was an old boy who lived in Sustead - he was known as 'Coconut' on account of the shape of his head, and I think he was partially blind, he wore big thick glasses; anyway, he used to go in the pub and play his accordion. He would come down from Sustead by pony and trap, and he always said he could get the pony down there, and it would get him home. Well, one night, some of the boys unhitched his horse, put the shafts through the gate, and then put the horse back on again. So when he got in and said, 'Go on!' nothing happened - the gate was there between him and the horse!"

Thurgarton Street

Tony Barber, whose family moved into Shop House in 1939, introduces us to the inhabitants of Thurgarton Street at that time.

Tony Barber "Mr. Spurrell was the team-man with the horses, they lived in the cottage opposite us, then the saddler Ted Sexton and his wife; further up were the Pikes, and they were all employees of Hammond, then Walter John Mallett, who lived in the end, then the pub. All our drinking water came from the well at Walter John Mallett's; Father used to have to go over every morning with galvanized buckets and get drinking water for the day; we had a well with a pump at Shop House, but it wasn't fit to drink."

Nowadays we take mains water for granted.

Tony Barber "The funny thing is, when you think of the hardships of those days, we all used to go to Mallett's for water, but Mallett didn't have a toilet there, their toilet was up the road, and right down the bottom of a garden; and, of course, I can remember, as a small boy, seeing Mrs Mallett, it would be raining, pouring, coat, rubber boots, umbrella up, tearing up the road - it didn't do to have any stomach upsets!"

Tony was one of the children allowed in to watch Bob at work.

Tony Barber "I used to go into the Bull, because I was friendly with Bob (Farrow); he was a wheelwright, by the way, he made tumbrels, he was a very skilled man. He had a car, but the car was all jacked up, because he used the four wheels with the rubber tyres on to make the two tumbrels - farmers preferred them with rubber tyres. His wife ran the pub. There was just one room in the Bull, she used to go down to the cellar to get the beer; the barrels were on racks in the cellar, it was down two or three steps, and they served the beer from there. I used to go in there with my grandfather, and had the froth off the top of the beer, which Mother used to complain about! I was only eight or nine then, quite illegal."

The Sextons were quite elderly at this time.

Elsie Davison "There was Mrs Sexton the piano teacher, the old lady in black, we all went there for piano lessons, poor Mrs Sexton; and Mr Sexton had the saddler's shop there, he was a sturdy man, a quaint couple, but there, they did their bit."

It would appear from our researches that Ted Sexton was the last exponent of the leather trade to work in the locality.

Tony Barber "Ted's workshop was never cleaned up, he had a wonderful collection of tools, what happened to them I do not know; he worked right through the war - he was very necessary, there were horses on the farms, he mended collars and straps; he mended canvases that went on the platforms of binders, he was a very good saddler."

Learning the piano with Mrs Sexton had its moments.

Phyllis Whitney "She was a scary old lady all in black. Her cat used to walk across the keys. She used to love lemon sherbets and she played the organ at Thurgarton Church."

Tony Barber "They had very little heating in the place - Mrs Sexton used to teach piano, I never knew how she managed to be so successful, because in the wintertime it was so damn freezing I don't know how the pupils could get their fingers to move over the keys."

Between them, Mr and Mrs Sexton made a memorable contribution to the services.

Tony Barber "Mrs Sexton played the treadle organ at Thurgarton. You never had more than half a dozen in the congregation in those

The Saddler's shop, Thurgarton

Emily and Ted Sexton

days; and Ted used to lead the singing - he had the most diabolical voice! *(chuckles)* You know Thurgarton church - it's a big church, it echoes well!"

The Chapman Family of Low Farm

Low Farm was a small mixed farm run by the Chapman family. There were five children, three of whom Paul, Billy and May, never married, working the farm together when their parents became elderly. They had a milk-round.

Tony Barber "At one time they used to go round delivering milk, they'd go round with churns on the handlebars of their bicycles! Each churn would hold three or four gallons, it was quite heavy, they'd hang it on the handle-bars; at that time there were no bottles of milk, they had a measure, they'd dole it out into your jug."

Altogether they are remembered as being hard-working and devout, with a strong affiliation to Thurgarton church.

John Neill has fond memories of the Chapman family.

John Neill "Hedgecutting, that was another big thing, we used to do all the banks by hand, with a hook, again, that was all done by piece-work, we were fairly lucky, we have grass hedges about. The Chapman family who farmed down in Thurgarton, used to come and clear out for us, they had cattle, and they had a milk-round; the Chapmans are all buried inside the churchyard here, there were three brothers and two sisters, I think, very religious people, they had a small farm, and they used to come and collect our grass trimmings up for their cattle; that suited us down to the ground, they were very nice people."

In later years, after Thurgarton church had been declared redundant, Paul Chapman became churchwarden at St Mary's. Canon Charles Bayes was always very moved by the evident depth of his faith. Ruth Bayes recalls:

Ruth Bayes "My husband always used to say that when Paul read the Gospel at Christmas, you felt as though he knew all the shepherds by name."

Merger of civil parishes

This took place in 1935, and at the next election of the Parish Council there were representatives from both parishes.

Throughout this period John Brown, carpenter, was the Parish Clerk.

David Cooke "He was rather austere, he was not one you got to know or got close to; all I remember is that I was once in his workshop using a plane - I must have been quite young at that time - and I was really enjoying it, I suppose I'd got my tongue out and whatnot, and there were these shavings whistling off the wood, you know, and he said, 'Master Cooke, it's not what you take off, it's what you leave on!'"

Note For many years of the century there were three separate Chapman families in Aldborough and Thurgarton

Chairmen of the Parish Council

1916 Dr Spurrell
1919 Joe Hulls
1937 Margaret Lilly

The Aldborough and Thurgarton WI

The Aldborough and Thurgarton WI was formed in October, 1918; Mrs Lilly was elected President, and Mrs Davey Vice-President. It quickly became a thriving group - which came to write its own award-winning history.

Aldborough & Thurgarton WI in 1923. Lady Suffield with shield.

On the facing page we have reproduced a page from the WI History from which we have drawn substantial information for this book. It is written beautifully in the hand of Phyllis Eddy.

WI History In the early days, the WI won Lady Suffield's Shield at the Norwich exhibition three years in succession, and were given a special certificate to commemorate it. It has many sub-activities, such as Country Dancing, Basket-making and Rushwork, and every year now it works for the Hospitals and Distressed Areas. It has been very successful in the drama competitions, has won the Folk Dance Shield outright, and has since that twice won the Folk Dance Bowl. These successes are mainly due to the enthusiastic leadership of Mrs Gay, who also runs the basket class. The WI has also been most successful in Co-operative Handicraft and Produce Exhibits, the most outstanding of the former being the Children's Altar in Aldborough Church. Miss Grimbly is the very efficient Exhibition Secretary. The WI is proud to have Lady Suffield, President of the Norfolk Federation, as a member. In June, 1937, this book, which was written in response to an appeal to every Women's Institute to record the history of its village, was sent to be judged by the High Sheriff of Norfolk, Mr Cozens-Hardy. It was placed fourth in order of merit; its record of houses and their inhabitants being particularly commended.

Aldborough Green was chosen as the site of the Coming-of-Age celebration of the WI movement in Norfolk, and staged The Dickens Fair and Pageant on the Green. Here is what happened.

1937 — 1938
The Dickens Fair and Pageant.

The chief event of this year was the Dickens Fair and Pageant held on Aldborough Green to celebrate the Coming-of-Age of the Women's Institute movement. It took place on July 21st. and 22nd., but unfortunately the whole event was marred by rain which fell almost unceasingly throughout the first day, and the second day was cold and damp. Thousands of women from Institutes all over Norfolk came to join in the County's celebrations and shewed a cheerful spirit in spite of the weather. Many wore costumes of the Dickens period, and the Green presented a busy scene with a street of shops built in the same period. The Red Lion changed its name to the White Horse Inn for the occasion, and the host and hostess, Mr. & Mrs. J. Harmer, played their parts well in receiving the company for the opening ceremony. Lady Suffield welcomed Mr. Pickwick, Mr. Tupman & a crowd of their friends, and she received a Victorian Posy from the Aldborough & Thurgarton W.I. The speeches made in London by Lady Denman, Chairman of the National Federation of Women's Institutes, and others were heard from a broadcasting van on the Green.

The street of shops included the Old Curiosity Shop which had for sale six articles sent by Queen Mary, Patron of the Pageant and joint-president (with Queen Elizabeth) of Sandringham W.I. Aldborough & Thurgarton were in charge of a Basket Shop, many of the baskets being made by the Class run by Mrs. Gay.

Our members were also responsible for providing the waitresses for the lunches and teas served in the Church Room.

Aldborough & Thurgarton Basket Stall.

Aldborough & Thurgarton W.I.

They all wore print frocks, aprons and mob caps. They also had poke bonnets to wear when their duties as waitresses were over. Mrs. Lilly, our President, was Vice-Chairman of the Pageant Committee, Mrs. Gay, one of our Vice-Presidents, arranged the Folk Dances, Miss Grimbly, our Exhibition Secretary, was the Performers' Steward, and the men of Aldborough and Thurgarton were given a great many duties to perform in connection with the Scenery for the Pageant, Bowls Tournament, & Car Parks.

Mr. Pickwick.

Village Talk

This short section is a miscellany of memory and random information which has no home but here! First, farming in the early years.

Gladys Miller/Dorothy Day "Years and years ago, there was an old drover and his dog used to bring the cattle from the market at Norwich by road on the Sunday - they used to rest on the Green. I can remember seeing, where the cattle walked, there was blood, because their hooves were bleeding, walking all the way from Norwich; and the old drover would stop and go to one of the pubs and have a drink or some refreshment. He'd walk all night, getting to Aldborough just as we were coming out of church."

Cyril Bacon "My father used to work at Manor Farm with horses, when he first came out of the army; Dunham was the farmer worked for. They used to go to market, and they used to buy cattle, about here; he used to take them up to Norwich, go through Norwich, down to Diss with 'em, used to walk them by road, all the way... up through Aylsham street, through Norwich, right down to Diss, to the market; they would be sold; he'd buy some more, that wa'n't quite so good, and they'd walk them home, and they used to start away at three in the morning, I heard him say, and they used to git home just gone after midnight. The old farmer, he had a pony trap, and he used to ride behind, and if they wanted a rest, he'd let them sit in the pony-trap a little while. I said to my father, I said, 'Well, how did you get on going through the town, didn't they want to run away like that?' And he said, 'It wa'n't no different to being on the ordinary road, he said, 'but they were nearly knocked up anyhow, they hadn't got a lot of strength to do a lot of running!' Which is right, isn't it?"

Elsie Davison "The harvest, helping with the harvest was the only thing we ever did in the holidays in my time, we all went to help, gleaners in the harvest field; we had sticks to run the rabbits, the boys used to go 'holdyering', didn't they; when they were carting the corn, the boys used to sit on the front horse and said 'Hold yer!' as they kept collecting the 'shoofs' (sheaves) up."

WI History When harvest was finished the farm labourers used to come to the trades people and others for 'largess', and had a harvest frolic at one of the inns, roast beef, plum pudding,, and of course drinks. This came to an end early in the Great War.

Life around the Green.

Cynthia Greene "In those days we used to put pig's fry and that in a tin, and take it down the bakehouse to put in the oven to cook. You used to go and put your meat in their big oven, pay so much for cooking it. People used to take their turkeys to cook in it too. And another thing, we used to have a coal copper, and we used to burn all the old cycle tyres Monday mornings, we used to smoke Aldborough Green out!"

A delightful photograph taken during this period of John Brown and Leslie Kent airborne along Yarmouth seafront!

Early sports on the Green - Penfold can be seen in the background.

The WI History is always a reliable source.

WI History Watch Oak. Here there was an oak tree, long since felled, which smugglers used to climb to watch signals from Cromer indicating that a cargo had been landed. The carts used to bring the kegs to Hilton Hill beyond the boundary of Aldborough, whence they were distributed. On the opposite side of the road is a small covert, which has been spoiled through road-widening.

WI History The name of Aldborough used to be spelt 'Alborough'. The 'd' was inserted by Revd R. Shuckburgh to avoid confusion with Alburgh and was adopted by the Post Office.

WI History Thirty years ago, a young man accidentally shot himself at the feu de joie outside the Red Lion after the wedding of Miss Nancy Wilkin, the proprietor's daughter.

WI History Mr A.J. Colman of Aldborough and Mr J. Knights of Thurgarton drove the first steam-driven car here in 1906. It took over twenty minutes to start it going..

WI History On a Saturday night of June 1931, there was an earthquake in England, felt mainly in East Anglia. Many chimneys were affected here, and many buildings violently shaken.

Now for a snippet about the school. In her recollections of her schooldays, Ida Impson recalled a teacher who was memorable for two reasons; one, the length of her stride, and two, her habit of reading as she walked along. We've found out who she was! Betty Crouch has been researching the history of Hanworth.

Betty Crouch A schoolteacher Lizzie Perks lived at the Homestead for many years until she died. She taught at the small Hanworth school which closed when the new large school at Aldborough opened in 1907. Lizzie Perks and the Hanworth children moved to the new school. Lizzie walked back to the Homestead each day for lunch with Sarah Suffling, then returned to school again. This was quite a lengthy journey across fields which were often muddy. She had a long stride and always read on her journey!

And the following memory of the aging Joe Hulls.

Gwen Coghlan "He was a funny old boy, Joe Hulls, he'd cut a hole in his hat, to let the air in, and he'd cut holes in his plimsolls to let the air in, he was a strange old man…"

Miss Perks & Miss Suffling

The School

Second selection of school-log

Harry Varden "I well remember the children from 1926-30, most of them wore clothes that had been around for a long time; patched knees, let-down trousers, and darned jerseys were normal for the majority."

December 3, 1928 In connection with the scheme for practical instruction, an intensive poultry house has been built locally to our design, and six pullets purchased from school funds. The management of the birds will be undertaken by the B+ children in rotation, and the work will be associated with the school garden instruction. Local poultry farmers who offer employment to boys on leaving school are interested in the scheme and expert demonstrations are being arranged.

December 4 & 5, 1928 Performances of the fantastic operetta 'Tangles' (Lollipop Land) were given by 60 children of this school in the Church Room at 7.30 pm. Large audiences assembled each evening.

December 12, 1928 Wintry conditions continue. Rooms this morning had average temperature of 32 degrees F., and it has been impossible to find satisfactory conditions of warmth during the day. It was decided to keep in the fires in the two rooms overnight, to ensure a better action of the hot water pipes.

April 18, 1929 First anniversary of Miss Earl's death. Children sent wreath to Thwaite churchyard.

August 14, 1929 School Flower Show and Exhibition. A very successful event was carried out by the staff and the scholars for the fourth time. There was an unusually large attendance. Following the displays of physical training and country dancing, Mr Harry Proudfoot, a member of the Education Committee, presented over 300 prizes. Teas were served by the staff and helpers during the afternoon, and a good programme of sports carried out by a committee of Old Scholars, in which house rivalry was keen, the Grecians defeating the Persians by 74 points to 69 points.

May 22, 1930 A short, simple ceremony was held in the playground, at 9.45am, to mark the significance of Empire Day. A chief feature was the hoisting of the flag, and the march-past at the salute.

September 15, 1930 In consequence of the state of the school garden after 5 weeks' holiday, advantage was taken of the weather, and weeding etc. was substituted for the ordinary, routine lessons this afternoon.

June 24, 1931 Re-opened after the fair. 66 children present out of 134. The weather which had cleared by 8.15am was probably made the excuse for keeping children at home, but the real cause lies in the fact that most of the children were attending the fair till 11 or 12pm and were too tired to be awakened for school.

December 21, 1931 The usual Christmas breaking-up party was held this afternoon. Following assembly, the classes entertained one another; then came a performance of 'A Christmas Carol', by the senior classes, as given in the Alby Parish Room the previous evening for their church Restoration Fund. There were a number of visitors, who assisted the staff in serving a bountiful tea to 140 scholars. Crackers, oranges and sweets followed.

June 16, 1933 The managers have been notified of the closing of Alby-with-Thwaite School, and the transference of the children there to this school after the summer holidays.

September 11, 1933 School re-opened after Harvest Holiday, five weeks. 26 children were admitted, of which number 20 were transferred from Alby-with-Thwaite school. Mr J. M. Hulls, Correspondent, visited.

September 10, 1934 It is with deep regret I report the death of Mr Guy Davey, Chairman of the School Managers, on August 19th. He was keenly interested in the progress of the school, and attended every function organised for the benefit of the scholars, invariably taking the opportunity of thanking the staff and their helpers for their efforts. It is entirely due to his enthusiasm for Health Education that we have the playing-field at a yearly rental of 2/6d.

September 29, 1934 A visit to London was made by 13 scholars and 2 ex-scholars under the direction of the Head Teacher and Miss Leeder. A very successful day commenced at 5am. and finished at 1.15am. The sightseeing included the Changing of the Guard at St James Palace, and visits to the House of Lords, Westminster Abbey and the zoo. Three girls became separated from the party at Regent's Park, and successfully negotiated their journey to Liverpool St. Station by bus and tube, on this their first London visit.

October 8, 1934 A wireless aerial has been erected, so that further experiments can be made in the matter of receiving broadcasts.

October 19, 1934 Attendance reduced by heavy rains. Hot cocoa is being supplied in the dinner hour to between forty and fifty children.

January 11, 1935 The milk scheme has been put into operation from the 8th inst. with an average of 42 bottles per day.

May 8, 1935 To mark the King's Silver Jubilee, a flagstaff has been presented to the school. An interesting feature of this gift is the co-operative nature of its presentation from the various parishes that serve the school. The larch pole was cut down in Hanworth Woods, prepared and erected by Alby and Thwaite, while the flag is being given by Aldborough and Thurgarton. It will be dedicated publicly on Empire Day.

May 24, 1935 Empire Day. A large attendance of parents and visitors watched the usual celebration at 9.30am. The flag and -staff were formally presented prior to the march-past and salute. Appropriate songs were rendered, and the Chairman of the Managers, Mr J. M. Hulls, addressed the gathering. Children and friends had added a plate, suitably inscribed, to mark the special occasion.

July 9, 1935 Board of Education report - excerpts
"This school comprises 4 classrooms and there is a gallery in each room. It stands on a site of one and a half acres, a small part of which has been let as a garden; a playing-field of 3 acres which adjoins the site is available by the courtesy of the owner at a nominal rent. The flower-plots around the school play-ground are in good condition, and the school garden is well-kept. The 155 children on books come from 8 parishes; the increase in numbers from 127 in 1933 was due to the closure of the school at Alby. It is an interesting fact that 6 council houses near the school provide at present 44 pupils. The teachers are on good terms with their pupils... 2 teachers, with 55 of the younger children, work in one room. An experiment has been made with the wireless this year.

February 14, 1936 An electric plug has been fitted to Room 1 (Senior), in order that wireless may be used to greater advantage. The source of supply is from the school house, the Head Teacher having indicated his willingness to pay for the current consumed. The wiring is by means of an underground cable from house to school.

March 9, 1937 Dr Green concluded the routine medical inspection. The correspondent to the local Care Committee (Mrs Eddy) visited at noon, and several log-book cases that needed following up were discussed with the Head Teacher and Dr Green. Malnutrition was evident in some cases seen. Two children, 11-12, were examined during the afternoon under Mental Deficiency.

Mattie

We close this section with a nostalgic piece that appeared in Norfolk Fair magazine in 1976; it was written by J. J. Maling, grandson to Joe Hulls. It harks back to an era in the life of Aldborough and Thurgarton which disappeared for ever through the changes brought by the increasing speed of mechanisation and the onset of the Second World War. (Joe Hulls died in February, 1940.)

When Grandfather retired, he moved into a comfortable house which was within sight and sound of the school, and I fancy there were times when Mr Carter, the new headmaster, wouldn't have minded if the distance had been greater. It was some months before Joe Hulls got out of the way of strolling into the school at odd times and taking charge again.

Yes, Joe ran most things. Of course, he didn't compete with the Barclays of Hanworth Hall, or the Suffields of Gunton Park, or similar aristocrats. They had their own place and duties, which were ceremonial and financial. They were allowed to open flower shows and contribute to good causes of every description. People would ask an aristocrat to open a show, but if they wanted one organised, they came to my Grandfather. He also provided an advice service, legal and otherwise, though he usually delegated the occasional tricky questions of disputed parentage to his wife. He gave practical help where he could and he had more clients than a Norwich solicitor. He collected chairmanships and secretaryships as others collect old china, many of them county-wide, rather than purely local. He was also the editor of an extremely nasty magazine with a greasy blue cover called IT, which stood for Independent Teacher. IT spent most of its time lambasting the Norfolk Education Committee and fighting off proposed libel writs. Believe me, Private Eye is fifty years behind the times. Eventually they made Grandfather a member of the Education Committee himself, and IT first grew respectable, then died of boredom.

He ran three friendly societies, Oddfellows, Foresters, and one I forget, and acted as accountant for many local farmers, as well as being official company secretary to the principal village shop, Bone & Co, grocers and drapers. As often as not he was paid in kind, and it was in some deal of this sort that Mattie his pony turned up, complete with pony trap and harness. Certainly he didn't pay for them, and the pony never cost him a penny for feed all the time he had her.

Mattie was the fattest pony I ever saw, and eventually the oldest, too; she lived to be thirty-four. She was a hollow-backed grey, with a sweet and rather playful disposition. Grandfather always used her for his frequent journeys to Aylsham for Council meetings and attendances on the bench. Mattie was a nice judge of what was right for an occasion. The Sunday excursions with my grandparents aboard were leisurely, with many a stop for mouthfuls of grass by the roadside, or friendly scuffles with the dog, Jack, which ran under the trap, gipsy fashion. She was seen at her best, however, when Grandfather went into Aylsham, especially in the years when he was Chairman of the Council. Then she pranced proudly along, well aware that she was heading for the North Norfolk equivalent of the Lord Mayor's show.

But age creeps up on us all. Grandmother died, Joe Hulls himself grew frail. Only Mattie seemed to be the same as ever; and she now spent most of her time grazing at the expense of a farmer down the road. "Old Joe's done my tax papers for twenty years," he once told me. "So I reckon I can spare his old pony a bit of grass." But death came to her, too, I can't remember how. It certainly wasn't from starvation.

During the Second World War
1939 - 1945

Air Raid Precautions   82

Evacuees   82

One Family's Story   85

Fire Watchers   86

The Home Front   87

Of Bombers & Bombing   90

War Talk   92

Margaret Lilly   94

Air-Raid Precautions

From the account in the WI History, Aldborough seems well-prepared for the war that was declared on 3rd September 1939. Here are listed some of the measures taken over the previous months.

WI History During the week of the September Crisis 1938, gas masks were delivered to Aldborough and Thurgarton, and distributed. In October, Mr Amis, ARP Officer from Cromer, gave a course of lectures on Gas, and issued certificates to those who attended. In November, Dr Eddy gave a course of lectures in First Aid, and eighteen members of the class gained British Red Cross Society certificates. The wardens were given a course by Mr Hawes, of St John's Ambulance Brigade. Mr T. Cooke was Chief Warden and Mr Harden Senior Warden. The canvassing of every house for the Government Evacuation of Children Scheme was undertaken by the Revd H. A. Stead, Mr R. Harden and Mrs Eddy, and met with a ready response. In May, an ARP Demonstration was held on the Green - aeroplanes flying low, bombs exploding, wardens in full, gas-proof clothing, dealing with the explosions, and members of the First Aid point attending to the casualties.

Some familiar names feature on the Parish Council.

WI History The Parish Council elections took place in March 1939, and the following members were elected; Mrs M. Lilly (Chairman), Dr J.A. Eddy, Mr W.T. Spurgeon, Mr A.J. Colman, representing Aldborough, Mr B. Hammond, Mr A. Chapman and Mr R. Williamson representing Thurgarton, and Mr J.S. Brown (Clerk).

Evacuees

Everything was in place for the arrival of the evacuee children the day after the momentous announcement.

WI History Great Britain declared war on Germany on Sunday, September 3rd 1939, and Aldborough and Thurgarton received 164 evacuees on September 4th. There were 75 children and 15 teachers and helpers from Dagenham, and 63 children and 11 teachers and helpers from Gravesend. They had travelled by boat to Yarmouth, and thence by motor-bus to Aldborough, where they were received at the Church Room and billeted in small groups among the householders. Mrs Lilly was Billeting Officer, but had no occasion to use her powers of compulsion. The Dagenham children attended the Aldborough Council school, and Gravesend School was accommodated in the Church Room, in which a second heating stove was installed for their greater comfort. The Temperance Hall was used by the Dagenham boys as a Recreation Room.

The children and their teachers were soon assimilated into village life.

WI History During the autumn, two concerts were given by the children, including a choir of twenty boys trained by Mr J. Fraser, Dagenham Music Master.

This choir, which practised in Aldborough Church on Saturday mornings, provided the Social Half Hour of the WI birthday meeting in October, and sang for the Carol Service in Aldborough Church on Christmas Eve. Our own children joined with the visitors for the concerts, which consisted of plays, songs and solos, and revealed much talent. The Church Room was filled to overflowing, the proceeds were used to give Christmas parties to the children and their foster-mothers. They were given a cinema show in the Temperance Hall, followed by tea in the Church Room.

Their stay was rather shorter than had been initially expected.

WI History There was a steady return home of the children and on June 2nd, when these villages were made a neutral area, there were only 43 children and one teacher to be re-evacuated, six of these went to their homes, two remained here, and the rest were sent to the Midlands.

Rose Purdy (née Wiseman) gives a reason for this.

Rose Purdy "They were moved on when it was decided that the airfields in the area made it a risky place to be."

However brief their stay, it is clear it made a huge impression on both parties, the children, and their hosts. Over thirty years later, in the school year 1988/9, children from the Primary School undertook a project on World War Two, including research into the evacuees who had come to Aldborough and Thurgarton. They managed to trace a number of people, who wrote back with memories of their time in Norfolk. The following children were involved with this project: Samantha Clarke, Tracey Cubitt, Tom Ash, Toby Mendes-Houlston, Daniel Wright, Josceline Hunter, Liam Murray, Tanya Chadwick, Sarah Thomas and Laura Bailey. From the replies to their enquiries, they compiled a fascinating booklet, from which we are able to quote now. They state:

In the school log book there was evidence that 244 children were evacuated to Aldborough in 1939. 119 came from Dagenham, 92 from Tilbury. By writing to London newspapers we managed to contact some of the people who came to Aldborough and other places in Norfolk. This book contains some of the letters they sent back to us.

We are able to include extracts from two of these letters.

Evacuee *(name not given)* The four of us in my group arrived at Thurgarton Lodge to stay with Mr and Mrs Harden. Our bath-towels had our initials embroidered on them. I spent my sixth birthday there and have photographs taken in the garden. I also remember Ethel and Dorothy, the two maids in the house. They wore either a blue or black dress in the mornings and a maroon one in the afternoons.

I think I was rather a difficult child, as I was moved on to stay with Mrs Stanion in Forge (or Stable) Cottage. I wasn't happy there and I remember an accident with a grandfather clock. I moved on to stay with the Daniels in their cottage next door to the Red Lion. They were very kind and I understand they died only last year.

James Allen lodged with the Dennis family, who lived in the isolated cottage that stands on the road leading to Hanworth from the former police house. He enjoyed a more settled time and his recollection is rich in detail.

James Allen We went in a car to Mr and Mrs Jack Dennis, Tweenways, Thurgarton. Our new family was a small lady named Marjorie - she had dark hair and eyes and was softly-spoken, a very big man named Jack and his father, Grand-dad Dennis. We had time to look around the garden which had many fruit-trees, chickens and three dogs. We were shown the strange-smelling little house at the end of the garden which was the toilet, how to draw up water from the well and the outside shed which was to serve as our wash-room. I think we first met Jack Dennis about tea-time that first day. He was a self-employed builder/handyman/chimney-sweep. He shook each of us by the hand; his hands were huge and showed signs of hard

83

manual work. I see him now dressed in a blue bib and brace overall and a thick grey shirt with a peaked cap askew on his head. He looked as if he had been punched on the nose a few times and, of course, as a champion boxer of Norfolk, he had been! We sat that evening in the kitchen talking about our families and getting to know each other. The Norfolk dialect seemed strange to us as I suppose ours did to our hosts. Grandfather had the strongest accent; he came from either East or West Runton on the coast where his family had been fisher-folk. We later became used to his frequent trips away and the next day we knew we would dine off salt herrings, which even after soaking in water were still the saltiest food I think I have ever tasted.

The house was very cosy downstairs but the bedroom was cold. The oil lamp in the kitchen provided the sole illumination and I was surprised how bright this lamp was. We three boys were to share one big bed, but as John did not remain with us for long we were soon down to two. I do not remember how we enrolled into the local school, but for some time we only went for a half-day, the local children the other half, morning one week and afternoon the next. The walk to school seemed a long way, but I know now it was not too far. There was plenty of free time which we used to get to know the local farm, Hammond's.

The teachers started a youth club in Aldborough on the corner of the Green *(now the Community Centre)*; this opened about two nights a week and we played the usual games, table tennis, dominoes, etc but to a 'Townie' the walk home in the dark to Thurgarton was very frightening.

I remember harvest time in the field opposite Tweenways. A tractor was used with a binder and the corn in bundles was stacked all over the field. When the binder reached the centre of the field and the last part of the corn, all the rabbits were hiding in there and as they broke for cover the local boys and the farmworkers shouted to bewilder them and knocked them down with sticks. I was not used to this sort of behaviour; to me rabbits (bunnies) were fluffy little things in children's storybooks and not vermin and I thought it sad that they were being killed, not knowing that they represented a dinner to a farm-working family...

...The winter of 1939 was very severe, there was the deepest snow I had ever seen and our house was cut off for several days, roads disappeared and the surrounding countryside looked just like a range of snow hills. When the council workmen finally cleared the snow I walked all the way to school through a seemingly endless snow tunnel. This snow did not clear for a long time.

One weekend I went into Aldborough to the mill owned by the Cooke family. It seemed the whole village was there; the pond was frozen solid, a few people possessing ice-skates were gliding around but we others made fun with very long slides on our boots and shoes. The ice was so thick that at one stage someone even dared to drive a motor-lorry on it!

And evacuees still make return visits and reflect on their life experiences.

Roy S. Harriss On September 5 1939 my brother and I were evacuated from Ford's Jetty, Dagenham on the paddle steamer Golden Eagle, taken to Yarmouth then on to Aldborough Green. My brother Derek and I lucked out by being taken in by Mr & Mrs Gibbons, who occupied the tallest house on the Green *(Chesterfield House)* ...to us Londoners it was a whole new life and 'game' to us, country lanes to walk, right of way across the fields, bird-nesting, helping hay-making; but the biggest thrill was the many trips in the trucks (sorry, lorries) that Mr Oliver Cooke used at his mill; they were big vehicles, nearly all Studebakers - either American or Canadian - and powerful. Derek and I had our favourite drivers, Ted Knight, Jack Daniels, and Almer; we had wonderful run outs all over Norfolk delivering all kinds of corn, wheat, flour, cattle-feed. The memory of those days will never fade, after 62 years - the school, Alby Hill, the homemade raft of wood we'd paddle down the millstream, pigeon-shooting, the Negro minstrel shows we put on at the village hall near the Red Lion pub, the rare visit from London of our folks who came by a special bus and were dropped off on Route 140 where the old sub post office was… Lots of good folk put their arms around us kids and warmed to us; I for one will never, ever forget those most turbulent and exciting days. My brother is in business in Tasmania, Australia; I have done well in the USA, and fly one of my four aircraft for retirement pleasure…

One Family's Story

We are familiar with many wartime stories which tell of the impact of war on people's everyday lives, in terms of personal safety, but here is a story that highlights the financial consequences of war on some families. Through the 1930s Sidney Barber and his wife ran a prosperous grocery business in Aylsham, but in the autumn of 1939 Sidney came to work as an employee of Bone & Co., for whom he worked as a roundsman. His finances had suffered a sudden blow at the hands of the bank. His son Tony tells us how it happened.

Tony Barber "We came to Thurgarton in November 1939, at the outbreak of war. Father had a grocer's business in Aylsham, where he was supplied by a wholesale grocery firm, Halleck & Bond in Kings Lynn. He had a monthly account with them - and they wanted their money in seven days! The banks simply foreclosed on all accounts, just like that - they just didn't want to know! Father went bankrupt for £450, which meant we lost a private car, a van and a house in Hungate Street for that money. And when it came to the bankruptcy court, there were four other little grocers who were bankrupt at the same time, all caught in the same trap."

The only option for Sidney Barber was to move to Thurgarton.

Tony Barber "W.H. Copeman, wholesale grocers, who owned Bone & Co., took Father over, and gave him a job; so we moved to Shop House, Thurgarton. And they were able to take Father on, because they had a chap by the name of Alma Harmer who'd been called up. So Father who had originally been apprenticed to the grocery trade, did the rounds - he was used to that. He went out as far as Reepham, because he had customers of his own there, so he took them on as registered customers, which did Bone a lot of good."

Tony goes on to describe the way Aldborough's three general traders pooled resources during the war years.

Tony Barber "Now the 'pool' delivery. There was petrol for only one vehicle, so they used to deliver all their goods with the three men on the one vehicle - both Days' and Kents' had a big, lorry-type van. This is where I spent my boyhood, in the holidays, going out on the rounds. The van used to carry paraffin, too, it had paraffin tanks built underneath. On Wednesday Father delivered on his own, in his own vehicle, a little Bedford van CPW 352, it was virtually new; of course Bone & Co. still had a horse and cart at that time; a chap by the name of Ketteringham from Matlaske used to take that round, and he used to take groceries and so on down to Shop House for Elsie to sell, because Elsie had groceries as well as drapery to sell there. Thursday he had a day on his own, and he used to do Cawston and Reepham, and various others on the way, and Friday, I can't remember, and he had a half-day on Saturday."

Tony remembers a near disaster.

Tony Barber "I was with him in the van going towards Cawston in the summertime, when we were machine-gunned by a German plane. He pushed me down; we had a bullet through the roof of the van, it glanced off and out through the side window, the window was open, so we had a near one there."

Fire-watchers

The villages had to prepare against the threat of air attack; consequently a Fire-watching Post was erected on the top of Oliver Cooke's garage, and volunteers manned the post every night to keep a lookout for damage to crops. Oliver's son David remembers it.

David Cooke "Alongside the garage was a prefabricated place which was built by the N.F.S. (the National Fire Service) as an A.F.S. place (Auxiliary Fire Service) - a little Fire Station, manned by volunteers; my father, as you would have expected him to be, was Fireman-in-Chief! *(laughter)* The National Fire Service provided the fire engine, which was an American van-thing, which towed a special firepump. So it wasn't a red fire engine, but equipment supplied by the NFS. So there were lots of local men, who became volunteer firemen."

David recalls being involved, as a ten-year-old, in their training activities.

David Cooke "They had regulars who came out to show them how to deal with fires. As a youngster, I had to go into the Red Lion, right up to those dormer windows, and wait to be rescued by a fireman. One of them, Fred Hall, had to climb up the ladder and rescue me! To begin with, I thought it was great - there was a crowd of people down below watching things, they'd had the fire engine going with the jets of water, I felt ever so proud. But when the moment came, when I actually went up to the window and looked down and saw that Fred Hall was going to carry me down across his shoulders, down this ladder, I was scared stiff!"

Harry Varden was recruited into the fire-watchers.

Harry Varden "We were a motley lot! Ollie was in charge, Oliver Cooke - mind you, he'd got no more idea about it than the rest of the people - well, nobody had any idea, really. They ordered us on to a stack one night, because when the enemy come flying over, you mustn't let any flames show. So we were on this stack with these beaters - lengths of worn-out canvas hose on a pole. I don't know what would have happened to me if I had not had this pole, because I suddenly went through to where the flame was - my feet went in, I've a scar on my leg now where that burned... no-one knew about it really, I struggled off the stack and pulled the hot bit out of my boot, that was it, you went on with the job."

Shades of Dad's Army in all this, but comedy was a long way off when Derek Filby wrote his poem.

The Fire-watchers
Through the night our vigil kept,
Through the trees the wind it swept,
While the peaceful village slept:
All could rest.

No marauding enemies,
Nothing but the starry skies,
Reflect, in our weary eyes:
All could rest.

Enemies may come one night,
Drop destruction left and right,
Give us all a nasty fright:
None would rest.

Watchers, you are here to see,
That our homes are damage-free,
Our support for victory:
Give the best.

The Home Front

Reading about the war years as recorded in the WI History, we gain a sense of vibrant community activity, on many fronts. Here is a selection, starting with the autumn of 1939.

WI History The First Aid Point for Air-Raid Casualties was established at Dr Eddy's house, the staff being Mrs Eddy, Mrs Harden, Mrs Hammond, Mrs Mallett, Mrs Martins, and Mrs Stanion. These, with other trained First Aiders, and the Wardens, met monthly for practices under the guidance of Mr Hawes. A branch of the Local Defence Volunteers, later called the Home Guard, was formed in June. Mr Harden resigned his place as Senior Warden to undertake duties with the Home Guard, and Mr John Brown took his place. The WI organised weekly work parties which provided knitted comforts for the Norfolk Territorial Army, the British Expeditionary Force, the Royal Air Force, and for the Christmas parcels for the men gone from the village to serve in His Majesty's Forces. Clothes were also made for the evacuees and for the refugees from Finland.

The Aldborough church bell was rung at midday as a call to prayer for Peace until June, when the ringing of church bells was prohibited. An evening service has been held since the end of June.

Mr Osborne of the Green Bakery was given the contract to supply 1,000 loaves a day to the troops at Weybourne camp.

There are some affectionate memories of this huge operation.

Elsie Davison "Osbornes that was a busy trade during the war, he supplied the army, you would see all the little Army vans waiting to collect bread, it was marvellous, really."

Esmé Hurn worked for Osbornes during the war years, recruited as a driver to service the contracts won by her new employer.

Esmé Hurn "Charlie Jarvis took me on the bread rounds with him for a week, and then I was put on my own! I had to take 450 loaves of bread to the Grand Hotel in Cromer after driving on the road for a week - no driving tests in those days - and very narrow roads, for example, through Metton, past Hanworth Cross and up Marble Hill. We used to deliver to Stiffkey, Weybourne, Sheringham and many other villages. The biggest van could hold 650 loaves. There were also rounds with deliveries to individual houses and I would carry a deep basket full of loaves and a shallow one full of cakes and flour. One day the oven blew up, and poor old Bertie Osborne came out with his face all black. This was at the top of the Green. Doing the deliveries was considered 'war work'; we were issued with trousers as we were on Army deliveries, a sort of battledress - and some of the older folks in the village thought it was a bit flighty for a woman to wear trousers!"

In a letter, Freda Parker (née Osborne) recalls the work of her parents.

Freda Parker "During the war my father was exempt from military service as he was given the contract to supply bread to the military camps including Weybourne and Stiffkey. He continued with the 'Rounds', delivering bread to the villages, managing to run the business with an all-female staff apart from one senior citizen, Mr Garnett Brett! My mother 'did the books' every night, counting up the money and banking it in the village. Dad also went 'fire-watching' in a little 'look-out' situated on the top of Oliver Cooke's garage."

She writes of her parents' wartime friendships.

Freda Parker "One Sunday, some soldiers from the Royal Horse Guards Regiment stationed at Wolterton came to chapel, and Mum and Dad invited them home to tea. There began a great friendship which lasted until the regiment was posted to Germany, and we heard later that many men were killed. We certainly never heard from them again, apart from one. We had some very enjoyable musical evenings with the soldiers, as one had a lovely singing voice and another one played the violin."

Musical activities were already well established in the village through the Aldborough Choral Society, conducted by Dr Eddy.

WI History On August 8th 1940, a meeting was held in Mr A.J. Colman's house, to form a Choral Society. Dr Eddy was asked to be the conductor and weekly practices were held in his house. Eighteen members joined and their first performance - of "The Heavenly Pilot", a sacred contata by Joseph Elliott - was given on Sunday, October 20th in the Church Room.

Opportunities were offered to young people, too, through the Aldborough Youth Movement.

WI History Mr W.J. Carter was Chairman at a meeting in Aldborough School on April 23rd, when about 18 boys and girls attended. Recreative evenings were fixed for every Wednesday; the girls held knitting parties, 600 jam-jars were collected and washed and taken to the Preserving Centre. Six of the members joined the Home Guard, two the A.F.S. and several are Fire-Watchers.

Dances held in the Church Room proved enormously popular.

WI History In October Mrs Mallett organised a Dance, which was such a success that she continued to run dances every fortnight for soldiers and airmen stationed in the surrounding district. They asked for more and the dances became weekly events. In April 1942, they asked for still more and dances were held twice a week. The primary object was to give the troops happy evenings but incidentally £200 was raised during 1942. Mrs Mallett and her chief helpers, Mrs Martins, Mrs Hunn and Mrs Morgan never missed an evening, while Mrs Eddy kept up an unbroken record as pianist. Home Guard and Fire Watchers were entertained, and there were a few 'free' evenings for the troops. The rest of the money was given to hospitals, Norfolk Blind, Cancer Campaign, War Charities, stretchers and blankets for the First Aid Point, British Legion, Prisoners of War, etc. etc. A very good Broadwood 7ft. Grand Piano was also bought and given to the Church Room.

The WI played a huge part in community life; among other things, they set new records in jam-making.

WI History (1940) A preserving centre was established at Aldborough Hall and made 2,900lbs of jam, jelly and chutney, and bottled 381lbs of fruit. There was an exceptionally heavy crop of plums.

The WI president's husband, the Revd Christopher Lilly, wrote a letter to the evacuee children who had only recently left the district.

Revd Christopher Lilly I expect Mrs Norman will have told you that Aldborough made over 2,000lbs of jam this season, and a quantity of tomato chutney; we had four or five people in the kitchen here most weeks from September to November, and our drawing-room had two trestle tables covered with pots of jam. It has all been sold now to the shop in the village.

The following years did not quite hit the peak of 1940.

WI History In the autumn of 1941 the WI Preserving Centre made 1098lbs of jam, and in 1942, 2002lbs of jam and 192lbs of chutney.

But they had also been busy in other ways.

WI History The Knitting Party continued its good work and made 437 garments for HM Forces, the Norfolk and Norwich and Jenny Lind Hospitals. Seven parcels, each containing a pullover, cap-comforter, socks and gloves were given to men on joining up, and Christmas parcels were sent to those already serving. The village adopted a former resident, J. Bowditch, Prisoner of War, as next-of-kin.

They were quick to respond to Government initiatives.

WI History Aldborough and Thurgarton was the first WI in Norfolk to start, in May, 1942, the Meat Pie Scheme in response to the Government's desire that country people should have the same chance of extra rations as the townsfolk had by visiting catering establishments. The pies were made at the Green Bakery and sold every week in the Church Room by members of the WI and were much appreciated by the inhabitants.

True! Rose Purdy remembers those pies.

Rose Purdy "I remember that once a week the Women's Institute baked pork pies, which all the families were allowed to buy to supplement their meat rations. As I remember, they were the best I've ever tasted."

When looking at the school in the first part of the twentieth century, we have noticed the extent to which poor health among children was a big factor in their education. Low levels of nutrition also played their part, as the school log extract we quoted for March 9 1937 makes clear: 'Malnutrition was evident in some cases seen'. This was not just a local issue. School meals were introduced nationally at this time

WI History Negotiations for the establishment of a School Canteen were begun in July 1940, but it was not until August 1941, that the Education Committee approved the scheme and converted a playground shelter into a School Kitchen. It was opened in January 1942, to cater for 60 children under the supervision of the Headmaster with a staff of two, Mrs Dagless and Mrs Barnard of Hanworth. Meals are served on trays through the hatchway of the Infants' Room after a journey of 20 yards and sometimes, in frosty weather, a somewhat perilous ascent of three steps. Numbers quickly increased to a daily average of 100, and a total of 20,937 dinners was reached for 1942. The ordinary charge for a two-course meal is 4d, with reductions when more than two members of a family remain to dinner. All the work of preparing the tables in the class-rooms used as dining-rooms is done by the scholars. 217lbs of jam were made in the autumn, from blackberries and apples picked by the children.

Of Bombers and Bombing

The fighting took place overseas, but the bombing happened here. The overall effect on the village population of the airborne fight was huge; not only was Norwich a major target for enemy attack, but there was an allied airfield at Matlaske, just 3 miles away. In the early years of the war, aircraft were a daily presence.

David Cooke "This was a very, very busy and significant flightpath; I can remember as a child there were thousands of aircraft that used to get in formation up in the skies over here, and Cromer was their main point they used to go out from. They used to return this way, and of course they would crash, and bombs were dumped in these areas."

Disaster came very near; a bomber came down very close to housing, in the field opposite Wright's garage.

WI History One August night, (1941) a Wellington bomber crashed in Mr Spurgeon's field, on its way back from raiding Germany. All the crew baled out, with the exception of the pilot, who landed with his plane and found his way to the doctor's house, where he was treated for his very slight injury. The plane broke an electric light pylon, so the village was without electricity until it could be put right.

David Cooke remembers where he was that night - the fire station by his father's garage.

David Cooke "There was a siren that went off to call the firemen out, and I remember being there, quite late at night, with whoever was on duty - I probably shouldn't have been! There was such a commotion, just behind here, at the back of this field, where even today there are high tension wires that go across. Well, this Wellington aircraft, on its way back from a bombing mission in Germany, was in trouble; its engines had packed up and it tried to land in that field. It was pitch dark, of course, so for the pilot it was a wild guess totally, but, well, it hit those wires and burst into flames. So the firemen were called out to it. I know my father and others went across there and they tried to get near the aircraft which was blazing - they thought there were crew on. But actually, the crew had baled out between here and Cromer; the pilot brought it down and he was OK. He'd jumped out and he went across to the doctor's; he was injured, but not too badly, he was able to walk. But that was a very, very close one, it was an absolute miracle it didn't crash on the garage. The watchtower in the top of my father's garage was dead in line... And the next morning, when it was daylight, there was live ammunition scattered over the whole field; and as certain specialists from the Air Force said, 'Coming up here as you did last night, you took your lives in your hands, how any of this ammunition didn't go off and kill any of you, we don't know'."

Harry Varden, one of the fire-watchers, remembers the incident a little differently.

Harry Varden "There were fire-watchers on, and they were both asleep that night! They were in the roof of the garage - I think somebody told them about the plane! You see, people were tired out, weren't they, it was hard to keep awake all night - I didn't go to sleep very often, we had a little snooker-table, it was best to be playing snooker! It wasn't my turn on that night!"

And a member of the Home Guard has this to say about the crash.

Anthony Day "I used to go around with Ernie Impson - we had guns, of course we did - I nearly shot myself! We used to go up to Watch Oak... It used to be all right when you got on Home Guard, you got up on that corner where it's fairly high, you see the old Wellingtons coming in, coming back home. There was one crashed at the back of Billy Hammond's. Crash-landed in the night up the roadway there, bullets were going off there like billy-oh. The pilot came through to Dr Eddy's."

A few days later, disaster was even nearer.

WI History On September 8th, at 10.23pm, a bomb weighing about 2,000lbs, was dropped on the home field of Chestnut Farm, Thurgarton, making a crater 36½ ft deep and 54½ ft wide. Nine smaller bombs, weighing 100lbs each, fell on the Hanworth crossroads field of the same farm. (The plane was a Heinkel HE 111k Mk 11a.) The farmhouse and buildings suffered considerable damage, and many of the cottages in Thurgarton Street were badly damaged. There were no casualties. One child was buried in debris and a boy thrown out of bed, while an aged couple were blown from the front of their house to the back. The Civil Defences Services were in action very promptly, windows and doors were blown open miles away, and the explosion was heard in Norwich, twenty miles distant. The following morning the farmer extracted fragments of the bomb from the exhaust pipe of his tractor with a silver christening spoon, while his son picked up about 1cwt of bomb metal from the farmyard. In spite of all this, harvest work was in full swing by 8am, and lorries were out to cart the corn then lying in a roofless barn.

The Bomb-Damage Repair Squad were out early in the morning, and by night all windows had been made weatherproof and the tiles replaced on all the cottages in the vicinity. Thousands of visitors visited the crater, as it was proved to be one of the largest in the British Isles.

Here are some comments from those living in

Thurgarton at the time.

Billy Hammond "The bomb fell in between the farm buildings and the police house; the bomb crater was quite substantial - if the bomb had fallen on the road we should have been in real trouble, real trouble. The explosion blew the roofs off all the buildings to Chestnut Farm, including the house, where we were living. My sister had to be pulled out of the rubble. I can remember looking up from the bed and seeing stars, the stars above, so the roof had gone. The corn barn had priority when it came to repairs - even had priority over my father's house, which was just corrected a little bit until months later. There was one large bomb and nine small ones, all in line for Matlaske airfield."

Tony Barber and his family were living in Shop House (next to the branch of Bone & Co.).

Tony Barber "The bomb was dropped by a single Jerry plane that came over; he got caught in the searchlights at Sustead, where there was an ack-ack battery which opened fire on it, and it jettisoned its bombs. This 1,000 pounder landed in the field behind the farm, and luckily, the blast was taken by the stack; if it hadn't have been, we probably shouldn't be here today, it would have wrecked the whole village; it made a huge crater, which wasn't filled in till after the war. And there was soil in the road, 18" deep, never seen anything like it. As I said, it smashed windows, but it hurt no-one; I had an enormous basket of shrapnel, real murderous stuff; a large piece, 15-18 ins long from the bomb, went straight through the engine of a tractor which stood at the side of the stack. It did rather a lot of damage! There was about half a dozen incendiary bombs with it, which dropped between the police house and Hanworth, there were little holes in the field all around where they dropped. The plane scarpered, he got away rather quickly…"

No little inconvenience to Ben and Nellie Farrow in the Bull, either!

Tony Barber "The bomb did damage to the Bull, it set the beer up, and they had barrels and so on exploding over the next two or three days, because the blast had an effect, as it would."

And that wasn't the end of it that night! Further along the road to Thurgarton church, another plane came down.

WI History That same night a Wellington bomber crashed in one of Mr Donald's fields, but there were no casualties.
Tony Barber "The Wellington bomber belly-landed behind the police house, in Neill's field; he was limping home, and, apart from the pilot, they all baled out."

Other memories.

Anthony Day "The bomb fell the same night the Wellington come down, 'cos when Bert and I went up there, ol' Bob Farrow, he was sweeping the glass up and the mud an' all off the road there. Bert just said to him, 'We're now going to look at the Wellington aeroplane', and he downed tools and he got on his bike, he come up there with us - he didn't realise that it had gone down. I'll tell you exactly where, it was between the old police house and Thurgarton church; there's a field with a sort of dip in it. That come down and landed, that slid along right from the other side of the field before that stopped. When Bert and I went up there about six o'clock in the morning, we'd heard about it, you see, the crew were sitting on the wing, waiting for the motor to come and pick them up…"

War Talk

We now include various individual accounts of experiences in the villages in wartime.

Tony Barber "We had troops all around, they were in the village every night, they used The Horseshoes at Bessingham, and the Bull, and in Aldborough, the Lion and the Black Boys, they used to run short of beer… I used to go into the Bull, because I was friendly with Bob (Farrow). Very popular it was, the Bull, especially with the troop population we had, very high."

Connie Harmer "I biked from Erpingham, I'd been home for my half-day, and I was coming home along the Calthorpe road, and they were machine-gunning me; I kept coming until I got to theirs, and I chucked the bicycle down and ran off indoors, and she said, 'Whatever's the matter with you?' and I said, 'Them old Jerries are after me!' And of course we'd got a proper little house there that they'd made for us all to go in, so we all got in, and they dropped a bomb up Thurgarton that night. And another day, Charlie Jarvis and I, we were in the cutting-up room making sausages when they were bombing Norwich; you could hear the planes going over, you could hear the bombs dropping, an' that; in the end the old gentleman Spurgeon, he come in and say, 'It's time you bloody well come in!' he say. I said to him, 'They won't hurt us.' 'No, but they might see a bloody light.' So of course we had to pack up and come in."

Anthony Day "We was looking out of our front door down at Stone House one night, when they was bombing Norwich, we could see the searchlight beams up, see the old planes going down the beam; and all of a sudden, my word, there was a plane come right over the top of us firing tracer bullets; some of them went in that little old pond right against us; a bit more, a lot of us would have got shot, we was looking out of the front door…"

David Cooke "I lived at this time by the mill, and can remember standing up at a window; the moon was shining that night and Norwich had been bombed and a German aircraft, coming back this way, saw the moon on Aldborough Mill and opened his guns at it. It was bedtime, I had moved away from the window and this bullet came straight through and hit the chimney stack in the bedroom! It made a hole in that wall! I was only a youngster at that time and I thought, only two or three minutes ago I'd have been right in line of that bullet. I think my father and somebody else were standing outside talking - and of course, everything was blacked out - and they said this aircraft just swooped down, and the pilot thought to himself, "We'll have a go at this!" - rat-a-tat-tat, hammering away at Aldborough Mill."

Cynthia drove a taxi during the war years.

Cynthia Greene "I used to go and pick the airmen up from Matlaske camp and take them to Aylsham station at six o'clock in the morning. I used to come back from Aylsham station - the Peterborough train was supposed to get in at ten o'clock, but never got in till two in the morning. I used to sit there with no heaters in the cars, remember, half a potato to rub the windscreen with. I used to get home at two o'clock in the morning, lay under that car on a sack, knock the tap and let all the water out. I was going back for the six o'clock train, I used to get up at five and lay on that sack, and put that tap and fill that with warm water, then Leslie Kent used to come across the Green, 'Have you started yet?' We both used to go, you know, and 'cos you had to crank it up in those days, 'I can't go till I know you're started,' he used to say."

Army vehicles were a common sight.

Anthony Day "One of their armoured vehicles got stuck down the bottom of the Green, Ernie Impson tried to pull him out - he couldn't shift that, the blinking thing weighed twelve or thirteen ton; he couldn't pull that out. Two or three on 'em tried to pull it out, they couldn't pull it out; then all of a sudden they had to phone back to the camp, and they come here with a great old big lorry, with a tow-rope; he just stopped up near George's where the Post Office is now, got a big old wire-rope and he just hooked that on and started the old engine up, and that wound the wire up and that pulled that out as easy as wink."

Here's a story involving Dr Eddy and some very special tennis balls.

Billy Hammond "Late in 1939, Dr Eddy became a military information collector, as he went about his work; I was his runner; with him I went to Wroxham to meet a number of others doing the same job, all in preparation for a possible German invasion.

The doctor gave me messages from time to time in a tennis ball for me to deliver by bike to secret places four and five miles east and west of here. I delivered these balls into an area where you could hear them bouncing down and down; there were drainpipes, concealed from view, set in fairly high ground. He would instruct me to take a different route - for Northrepps I went by Thorpe Market sometimes, and Cromer other times. As a smokescreen, I had to be seen with the doctor, I went fishing with him several times; I remember him killing a fish by knocking it on the head with his big cherrywood pipe. He was the Captain in the Home Guard."

Margaret Lilly

Margaret Lilly was born in 1885 into the Gay family of Aldborough Hall; in 1914 she married Christopher Lilly, who had recently taken on the parish of Aldborough from his predecessor Mr Borlase. As we know, her elder brother Edmund was tragically killed in action during the First World War, leaving Margaret as landowner and lady of the manor. She had three sons, Denys, Geoffrey and Kit. Now from her mother she acquired the habit of writing a daily diary, a habit she maintained until her death at the age of 68 in 1953. Her diaries are a phenomenon! Each is of standard format, allowing her a half page for weekdays and a full page each for Saturday and Sunday. She wrote fully for most days, and supplied a summary at the end of each diary of key events of the year. You will shortly be able to read some excerpts, which will give a flavour of them all.

And what did she actually do to merit a road being named after her in the 1970s? Quite a lot! Apart from being a major landowner and wife to the Rector, she was at various times Chairman of the Parish Council and President of the WI; she was a school manager (termed 'school governor' today), she ran a youth group called 'King's Messengers', she was active in the Mothers' Union, she was Billeting Officer for evacuee children; as we have read, she hosted regular parties for the children from the village Sunday Schools at both St Mary's and the Methodist chapel and was committed to the maintenance of the Church Room throughout her life.

But what she did, came from what she was. Here are some comments from those who knew her.

Billy Hammond "Mrs Lilly was President of the WI when my mother was Secretary. She came by bike almost weekly to discuss WI business with my mother at Thurgarton. She biked everywhere from Aldborough Hall, with her big bicycle basket, always giving something to someone. She arranged big parties for people at Aldborough Hall, providing transport for those attending, with children always coming away with a present. She didn't drive, but she biked away, even in the greatest of gales; so unlucky for her to have talking troubles - a cleft palate, was that it? - but you could always understand her."

She practised a particular pastime.

Donald Colman "What everybody remember about her… she was a person for knitting, she had her knitting with her, if there was any parties on, she'd sit there knitting away in the dark; she only had one needle, she never did have two like an ordinary person."

She was tireless in offering practical help to people where she could.

Donald Colman "She used to go round in the wintertime to all the old people, or the poor people, she'd have a basket on the front of her bike - a sit-up-and-beg bike, a basket on the back, be full of rabbits, all ready for them to cook, vegetables too…"

And a final comment before the diary extracts.

Daphne Nichols "You couldn't have found anyone kinder."

Margaret Lilly's Diary

When I came to choose a particular period to include in the book, I decided to focus on six weeks in the summer of 1941, because I knew that the major incidents of the war, as far as Aldborough and Thurgarton were concerned, took place then. Given the scale of the diary material, I've had to make selections from her daily entries. Even so, the nature of the writer herself and the flavour of the times come through most strongly.

Aug 1 I took magazines in the morning; there were a lot of soldiers on the roads, and apparently Aldborough was infested by Germans! It began to rain as I came home but it cleared up at lunchtime. I bicycled to Gresham and did nearly three hours currant-picking.
Aug 2 Leslie Kent and Mildred Barrett married at 8am.
Aug 4 I collected War Savings and War Charity envelopes. Denys went off to fire-watch at 10.30 pm. No excitements.
Aug 5 Home Guard in Church Room. Cold and rainy, high wind. Nurse came to see me early, Norman drove me to Sheringham for the Board meeting at 11.45; we got back very early as there was very little business at the Council or the Housing Committee. Chris and I went to the hospital in the afternoon, and took lettuces to Nurse (and marrow)… I called in at Mrs Suffling after, as Nurse had told me she was unwell. I found her in bed and very miserable.
Aug 6 I cycled to Baby Weighing at 3, Mrs Wolsey's turn for taking it. Quite a lot of mothers and children and some visitors.
Aug 8 I went to pick currants at 11; on the road, Newstead and Joe Colman told me that a Blenheim bomber had crashed in flames in Barningham at 10 am. Two of the crew baled out, but the parachute of one failed to open. I took about half an hour to get to the far field by the pylons and picked till 5.15.
Aug 9 Priscilla and I did the church flowers at 10; Geoffrey rang up at 5.45 to say he was at Cromer station and would walk along the Norwich road. We all went to fetch him. After tea, we all went with Denys to get the tractor; and coming round the bad road between the Mansions and the Corner House, a bicyclist suddenly dashed round, obliging them to swerve up the hedge, and the whole thing turned turtle. Denys jumped clear, and managed to pull Geoffrey out before it could pin him. They tried to get Oliver but he was out, and they phoned here to get Chris to go again for him. They managed to rig up a pulley and block, got it turned up, and pushed it down to Corner House, Oliver arriving just as they had finished!
Aug 10 Double summertime ended.
Aug 14 Denys and Geoffrey cut oats in the Alder Carr, and barley in Cooke's field, and got 17 rabbits out of the latter. In the morning they cut the first wheat in Aldborough Road I, getting 5 rabbits. Dr Eddy came to lunch (Mrs Eddy being away for the inside of the week, to see her mother who has shingles). We gave him 2 young leverets shot in harvest, and a grapefruit tart. He didn't stay long. The boys rushed in and out. I had to go off and give out wool in the Church Room 2.30 till 3.15. I went to see Mrs Lee who has had a bad heart attack, and is still very ill. Chris went to see Brown to stir him up about a porch for the Church Room.
Aug 15 (Airgraph letter to Kit) Denys began cutting wheat in Hall Road III, but had to stop as the binder key blew out and broke; it also began to rain and continued for the rest of the day. Pentney mended it.
Aug 16 I bicycled to the village after with hollow biscuits for Mrs Suffling, who still has bad lumbago and to Mrs Lee who is no worse. Heard bombs in the night, a long way off.
Aug 17 Denys and Martin finished cutting

Aldborough Road III in the afternoon. We heard bombs again about 11.30pm.

Aug 18 I collected War Savings early, Chris went to see Mrs Suffling who is a little better, and enquired for Mrs Lee, who is very tired. Mrs Lambert at the Board was horrified that Mr Hammond had been working on Sunday.

Aug 19 The boys cut Aldborough Road IV and the 11 acres and started the Corner House field. I took tea to them at the Corner House. I went to see Mrs Lee, a little better, and Mrs Suffling who has so much pain in her legs now. I took a Red Cross apron to Mrs Eddy.

Aug 20 About 4 o'clock Martin phoned up from Corner House to say Denys had shot himself in the arm. I rushed down with bandages to find Nurse had been attending Mrs Gibbons and had done him up. I took him straight into Cromer, and we were lucky in catching Dr Fawkes at the hospital. He X-rayed Denys and said most of the pellets were in so deep they were best left in, but he got a few on the surface out. Denys had been getting the gun from under the cover of the tractor… and the hammer caught.

Aug 21 I bicycled to the Church Room to give out wool, and Mrs Eddy and I put up curtains behind the bookcase, but had not enough stuff.

Aug 22 I bicycled with a few ripe plums to Mrs Suffling, who is slightly better, and saw Mrs Lee, who is decidedly better.

Aug 24 I bicycled to early Service, and Martin and I took the Austin at 11. Denys couldn't get his arm into a sleeve, and didn't go to church. A lovely afternoon and evening, with a gorgeous sunset. Daisy came to lunch, and invited the boys to tea and croquet.

Aug 25 Mrs Lee died.

Aug 27 Another fine day and windy. Chris auto-cycled to the Lee's with the pall and to see Mrs Suffling in the morning. I bicycled to the church and tidied up the flowers and took 5/- concert money to Mrs Wilkin for piano and runner beans to Mrs Pope, Martins and Culley, and went to tea with Daisy.

Aug 28 The telephone rang at 3.30am. We found the electricity off and Oliver phoning to ask if we saw a fire Matlaske way. Denys saw a glow the village way, got Norman and they found a Wellington bomber had crashed just behind Spurgeon's; no-one in it, and they searched the fields in vain till 6.30, to hear later that the pilot had landed near the doctor and gone in there! They think the others are safe. The plane had crashed into a pylon, but they got it mended and the light on by 9pm.

Sept 3 Denys carted Big Wood II and part of the Alder Carr and Water-wheel fields, and also took the door from the cupboard in Geoffrey's room to Brown to be used for the porch to the Church Room. (ARP).

Sept 4 I took a pear to Mrs Suffling and went to the Church Room to give out wool for the work party. Brown has nearly finished the porch, made out of the Fair lavatories!

Sept 8 The boys carted barley in the Mansions field and finished a stack. About 10 o'clock we heard two sticks of bombs very near. Phoned Wickmere, all right, after looking round; then phoned the Hammonds and heard their windows were all blown in and ceilings down.

Sept 9 Bomb crater 55ft wide x 35ft deep. About 3 a.m. a Wellington bomber crashed in Mr Donald's field. All seven occupants were unhurt, and it did not catch on fire. I bicycled to the Hammonds, found lots of helpers getting things straight, talked to the inhabitants of the 'street' where most windows are broken, went to Villa Farm and saw the enormous crater in Mr Hammond's field just behind the house. I brought back blackberries from the school. Mrs Donald, White, Stanion, Carter and Morgan came in the afternoon, and we made 80lbs of blackberry and apple jam.

The Middle Years
1945 - 1975

Agriculture	98
Thurgarton	101
The Levelling of the Green	102
Giddybar	104
Traders	105
Fisher's General Store	105
Days' Stores	107
A.G. Davison & Son	108
Barclays Bank	108
Kents' Stores	109
Bone & Co.	110
Engineering Works	111
The Mill	112
Valentine's Day	114
Places of Worship	116
Eileen Hammond	117
Sport	120
Cricket	120
Football	121
Boxing	122
The School	123
Poultry Farm	129
The Over 60s Club	129
Doctor Talk	130
Aldborough Apples	132
Youth Club	133
Charles Matts	134
At Thurgarton Church	135
Aldborough Mill	138

Agriculture

In presenting a survey of a hundred year period in the life of a rural community, it soon becomes very clear that the sub-division into a group of decades is rather artificial, unless we are dealing, as we have just seen, with exceptional circumstances such as war. Otherwise, all we can chart is a steady evolution, with specific developments here and there to pinpoint change. This is particularly evident in any study of farming practices, where the underlying story has been the replacement of man- and horse-power by machine. The loss of horse-based activity and the trades associated with horses is crucial to the story of Aldborough and Thurgarton in the twentieth century. As a reminder, here are the words of John Brown, who himself wrote, probably in the late forties, a short survey of the changes he had witnessed.

John Brown A number of village crafts are vanished, such as: harness-makers, whip- and glove-makers, sawyers, colt breakers, curriers, tailors, horse slaughtering etc. In connection with the latter, there was a tannery for curing the leather, and the by-products provided grease for cart wheels, scrap-cake for game feed, bones to the bone-mill, and hair to make mortar for plasterers.

However, the process of change from horse to machine accelerated markedly in the few years following the Second World War. We can see this in the story of John Neill, who has farmed Thurgarton Hall since 1947, when his father bought the farm from his brother-in-law.

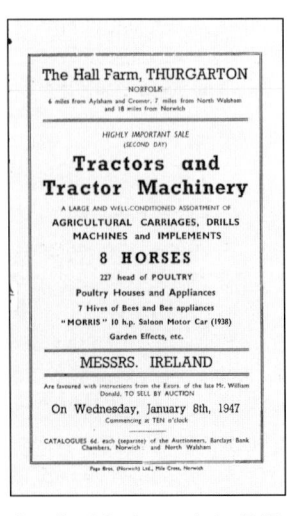

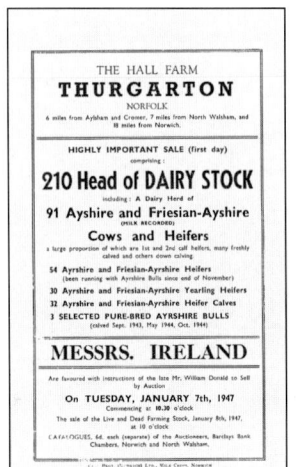

John Neill "We bought the farm in 1947, from Mr Donald who was my uncle - his wife and my mother were sisters, from Ayrshire, originally. I think Mr Donald came down in 1934, and I as a child came down and visited him; I can remember being taken down to the mill to see the ducks, so that's a long while ago - I was born in 1928. The mill was rather an attractive place in those days, lovely old place to visit. My father bought this place in 1947; my brother and I came down for the farm sale; I can remember that it was a very cold day, bitterly cold.

I was head cowman for the next five years, while my brother was the boss; when we took the farm over there was a lot of men on the farm (there were seven cowmen alone working for my uncle with his eighty cows); anyway, we were left with sixteen men on the farm. We didn't buy any of his cattle at all; we had an Ayrshire herd, while the cattle here were black and white, we were quite proud of our Ayrshire cattle. And as we built the herd up, my brother employed a fellow called Charlie, who, believe it or not, came from Alabama; he'd been left over from the war, a lovely man, super chap, never in a hurry, but was always prepared to work, do anything you asked him to. He was a good, big fellow. We retained

Details of the farm sale in 1947

the sixteen men the whole way through - some came, some went - but basically the men stayed with us. Early on, Kenny Amis took over as foreman. Now Kenny left school and worked with me on this farm all his life except for two years when he went into the Air Force, when he did his National Service. And his grandson Richard is now my manager; he left school and has come with me, and he's now, I'm guessing, thirty-six, thirty-seven.

I was the head cowman till 1951, when I became the boss, the farmer, I should say. At that time we were farming 406 acres, and today I've about 1,000 acres altogether; I've got four men, one of whom is full-time on the lorry, carting sugar beet, one is the manager, another does the ploughing, and the other at harvest time does all the drying - that's at the other farm at Matlaske, which I bought in 1965, I think it was.

When we came in 1947, we had six horses; one, Polly, I kept for a very long while, something of a pet, but we had a Land Girl, Helen, who used to feed the cattle with Polly; we had no tumbrel, so she used to sit on the horse and go out and feed cattle. Mainly Suffolk Punches, big, heavy, strong horses, quiet - not always, but most of the time. We had a stableyard here, and all the horsemen looked after their own horse. We were just at the change then, more tractors were coming in, and we didn't have horses for very long, they were very slow; we used them for drilling sugar beet, old Fred Barnard used to do that, he could steer it and keep it absolutely straight, he was a marvellous old boy. The horsemen would be here at half-past six - but I can't honestly remember too much about the horses, because I was in the cowshed, I was up early every morning. And by the time I took over in 1951, I don't think we had any horses left, apart from Polly.

John Neill outlines the main changes in crops.

"There have been big changes in crops - when we first came here, the main thing was sugar beet, wheat and malting barley, which was never a great money-spinner - there always seemed to be a competition, who could grow the best malting barley, but the figures just didn't add up, so we moved more into wheat; then we started growing potatoes - 1953 or '54, - with I think eight acres of potatoes. I cussed them the whole time they were there, said I'd never grow them again! But I went on, till I was growing 140 acres of potatoes. I did that for many, many years; I grew potatoes for forty years. For the last twenty-four years I grew them all for Walkers Crisps, I was very proud of them, and I got on well with Walkers, I never ever had a contract with them.

Then of course we went into vining peas in a very big way. Planted my first peas at about the same time, only five acres; but soon I had a contract with the Ross group, and it wasn't too long before I was growing a very big acreage of peas, which did exceptionally well. Oil-seed rape, that's another new crop, we try and help the texture of land, and get an early entry for wheat.

I sold my cows in 1967, when I bought the Matlaske farm; we're in an arable area, aren't we? Other things make more money, potatoes, for example… you know there was a tremendous demand for food at that time, but there isn't now; you couldn't produce enough of anything; from when I started just after the war, there's always been an opportunity to sell, but it's not like that any more, there's a lot of people suffering.

At that time, a lot of people ripped everything apart, vast prairies - maybe I'm one of them, I don't know, but I've put a big lot back. We planted a big lot of trees on the farm; my first trees were planted in 1952, but you never make any money out of growing trees. I felled my first wood - that was a poplar wood down at the bottom - I lost out there, but there's an amenity value, I'm pleased with trees, I've got some lovely little woods all round about."

Progressively, the smaller farms were absorbed into the larger holdings of the principal landowners, of whom John Neill of Thurgarton Hall is one. Another is the Hammond family, who started working the land at Chestnut Farm in 1920; Burrell Hammond farmed here until 1960, and his son Billy started soon after the Second World War. In his first years, it was a mixed farm. Here he tells a harrowing tale, concerning a dog attack on his flock of sheep.

Billy Hammond "I was in my early times of farming, that was a real tremendous blow, it's a story indeed; I'd come home from hospital (I had the use of one eye, the other was patched up a bit), went down to look at my sheep and there were dead sheep all over the place - that was real disaster. There were thirty-three of them, but how many lambs we lost we'll never know. I had great help from the village policeman John Lock, he was just a most wonderful man; he said these dogs must come from Bessingham, so we went round the houses, and took some samples with brown paper bags and caustic soda; these samples were sent to Birmingham police for analysis; two came back with sheep wool; the people who owned the dogs in question were spoken to, but they had no insurance, nor did I. About a week later, this same policeman saw sheep at Bessingham being chased by a dog; he knew where there was a 12–bore shotgun in a house there; on his bike he raced to the house, got the gun out and shot both dogs - the dogs that had been positive in the samples."

Mention of a policeman brings us to the recollections of Ray Spinks, whose father PC Edgar Spinks was village policeman from 1953 until his retirement in 1964. He gives here, in a letter, some background to the living conditions encountered by the Spinks family, and the reasons for the choice of location of the police house.

Ray Spinks We moved there from North Walsham, and it was something of a culture shock after being used to all the mod cons of a town. There was no electricity, running water or mains sewage when we first arrived, and our drinking water was obtained from a hand-operated pump, our lighting and cooking was provided by paraffin appliances, and as for the disposal of sewage, suffice it to say we had some of the best rhubarb in the area! After a few years, however, mains water, Calor gas lighting and cooking were provided, and the sewerage system was modernised, with electricity finally provided in the late fifties. The police house stood at Thurgarton crossroads, in a rather isolated position. Prior to the building of this in 1938, the constable lived in a private house just off the Green. Apparently, a new Chief Constable insisted on such houses being away from the village, so that the villagers could not see the officer's comings and goings - a ploy designed to prevent any person with criminal intentions knowing when he was out on his beat, or at home. Rumour had it that Burrell Hammond, who owned the land, did not particularly want to give up the piece in question, and offered some land closer to the village at a much cheaper price, but the Chief Constable was not to be moved.

Thurgarton

The bomb which landed in the field between the police house and Thurgarton Street blew the glass out of the shop window at Bone & Co., effectively ending its operation. However, after the war it was re-opened as a business by Joe Perrin, who had married Joan Tash, daughter to Mr Tash manager of the main shop on the Green. Rationing was in full force, times were hard, resourcefulness was called for.

Rose Purdy *"There's a tale about a boy who was having his hair cut, and telling Joe he'd just bought a cycle from Fisher's; the story goes that Joe threw down the scissors, and told the lad to let Mr Fisher finish cutting his hair!"*

Tony Barber "Joe Perrin was a character, he ran a hairdressing business, although I don't think he'd ever cut hair in his life, and he repaired bicycles, and he also made hair-cream, which looked a bit like Brylcreem, but I think he made it from lard, and it was the most revolting stuff possible; he did a roaring trade in that for a time, he used to collect up jars, because, again, you couldn't get jars, and his shop window, he had all these different size jars, with this hair cream in it, it was funny; he didn't last long, most people, once they'd been to have a haircut with him, they didn't come back a second time, he was good at plucking the hair out, rather than cutting it. And I don't really know where Joe went to, they split up and…"

Cutting hair was a popular choice of occupation when money was short.

Ray Spinks I remember having my hair cut in the bar of the Bull at Thurgarton, during opening hours, I might add, and if my memory serves me correctly, it was the landlord, Ben Farrow, who wielded the shears, in between serving pints. When the pub closed, we thought a trip to the barber would mean a journey to Cromer, but help was at hand in the form of Joe Perrin, who owned the cycle shop opposite the pub, and he took on the job of hairdresser. Now, instead of waiting while a pint was sold, it was a case of sitting in anticipation while a bicycle pump, or a tyre and a tube, were dispensed.

Photo courtesy of the EDP

The policeman John Lock is remembered for his prowess on the cricket field, too. And he wasn't without his Royal admirers! Billy Hammond tells the story behind this wonderfully evocative photo of youngsters playing cricket taken by the EDP.

Billy Hammond "The scene for that photo was all got together in a hurry. The game was put on for the EDP; they arrived, word went round and a few of us had to get out there just to have the photo taken. I'm the batsman at the non-batting end. There's John Lock, Dobbie putting his pads on, and Reggie Hunn, just behind Dobbie, and Robin Creasey's there too. Mr and Mrs Chapman from the Post Office. And this old boy was always about here, and he was Loynes; he lived down what years ago was called Curtain Row, (now called Thwaite Hill); he was a nice man who enjoyed cricket, a retired farmworker. The policeman was a very, very good cricketer, but he was missing from here a lot when the King came to Sandringham; he was a special policeman if ever there was one; he was the village policeman, but he was always taken to Sandringham, when the Royal Family were there. Yes, he was a special man."

The Levelling of the Green

The Green was in poor shape after the war, and the Parish Council determined to set about improvements. It was decided to level the Green. A new committee was formed to oversee the operation, from raising the finance, to engaging the contractor. Here is a contemporary account of one of the early moneyraising events.

Neville & Chapman inspecting the Green

Report on fête Aldborough village and district were in a large measure congregated on the Village Green on Saturday last when the efforts of the last few weeks culminated in the fête for raising funds for the renovation of the Green... among the attractions a Flower and Produce show was held in Messrs Kents' garage. At the same time a Rabbit Show was being held at the Red Lion garage attracting a large number of entries judged by Mr G.A. Twiddy of Mundesley and proved a great success. To the strains of music from the Aylsham Band, a programme of sports and country dancing, with a large assortment of sideshows and competitions entertained a large crowd till tea which was served by willing helpers in the Church Room. During the evening a programme of adult sports was the main attraction till the presentation of the prizes by the Hon. Doris Harbord at 8pm following which dancing was carried on till midnight. *(Abridged.)*

With money in the bank, the work was started. On September 27 1949, the EDP ran this report.

A Weird Monster at Aldborough Green
For hundreds of years the people of Aldborough have looked out over their village green, the scene for 700 years of the annual fair. Six acres in extent and almost surrounded with houses - no two of which are exactly alike - it formed a scene not often equalled. Readers may remember the fête held in the summer to raise funds to renovate the Green, which, owing to the fact that grazing had then ceased, had got very rough and untidy, making it unfit for cricket, football, or in fact for any other useful purpose. Now the work has started, and we have seen a weird monster towed by a caterpillar tractor tearing up the old turf in huge swiss rolls and dumping it in the low end where it is hoped the football pitch will be extended. Having first cleaned out many tons of mud from the pit and now clearing all the old turf off, the village youngsters are arriving home covered in mud or dust which has not seen the light of day for many centuries, and which it is hoped after re-seeding will not be seen again for many years.

The whole scheme was not without its controversies. One issue was the question of organised sport being allowed to take place on Sundays. One who protested was Mr Herbert Baldwin.

Billy Hammond "This man Baldwin was a very religious man, not church, he was chapel, and when cricket was played on Aldborough Green on the first Sunday, he just walked diagonally across the Green two or three times; I played that Sunday... He was a good man, I remember him well; he drove a lorry for Oliver Cooke during the war. In spite of being in the garage business, Oliver Cooke also had a wartime Government timber business, and Herbert Baldwin drove for him. That particular Sunday he walked across the Green and back, and then he did it again."

Another to oppose 'Sunday Games on the Green' was Fred Osborne, who had been Chairman of the Green Committee from the very start. For him, the issue was fundamental, and it led him to write this letter of resignation:

Fred Osborne As I have not now the confidence of the Green Committee, it is not right for me to continue as its Chairman, I therefore ask you to receive my resignation. Further, I was appointed to the Committee as a Representative of the Annual Public Meeting; it now seems the Green Committee intends to ignore the public opinion Re: Sunday Games on the Green, I therefore resign from the Committee.

The resignation was accepted with regret, Fred Osborne was duly thanked for his work, and Stanley Crame (recently appointed Headmaster at Aldborough School, following the retirement of Mr Carter) was elected Chairman. Another issue which caused wide upset up and down the lanes was the question of tennis. It centred on the establishment of grass courts which would require some kind of enclosure, the type of netting and the scale of concrete post required to create such an enclosure, and whether such netting could be allowed at the ends of the court only, or whether the sides might also be enclosed. The issue called into question the very nature of common land, and was debated endlessly in the Green Committee, and by Erpingham Rural District Council, and freely reported on in the press under the headline 'Aldborough Green Restraint Motion Rejected by R.D.C.' The article begins:

Aldborough Green, the rights of commoners over it, the interpretation of bye-laws about it, and the playing of organised games on it, were discussed at length yesterday by Erpingham Rural District Council...

The tennis courts did not survive very long.

Giddybar

Before we leave the topic of the Green itself, we will recall a man who decided to live on it, for months at a time, and for many years in succession. He was christened Albert Temple, but his name was Giddybar. His working life was spent as a jobbing carpenter on the Hanworth Estate, and his house, when he chose to live in it, was one of the brick and flint bungalows down near the Temperance Hall. It is said that when one of his daughters, Romany, married and needed somewhere to live, Giddybar moved out of his house next to the Green and into a caravan parked on the Green. He had a cunning plan.

Cyril Bacon "Well, they could come and park on there for one year, any time, and as far as I know, I'm sure it is, because Old Giddybar Temple had his caravan on there, and he used to pay the boys to give him a push up, so he shoved it up past the length of his caravan, so he could stay there another year, and he did; stayed there for years like that."

That's how to handle bye-laws!

Cyril Bacon "Well, he used to go in the pub with that *(his*

Minutes of the Green Committee

June 2, 1950
It was proposed we ask Mr Temple to move his caravan to a better position for the convenience of putting.

March 2, 1951 AGM
Mr Colman mentioned the good work done by Mr Temple in picking up papers etc. A collection was made which will be handed to Mr Temple.

April 25, 1952 AGM
Mr D Davison suggested we again recompense Mr Temple for his work in keeping the Green free from litter, by way of collection, as previous year. This agreed unanimously, and £1-12-7 collected and handed to Mr Temple.

October 22, 1954 AGM
It was stated that owing to illness Mr Temple would be unable to continue picking up litter. Committee agreed we try to get someone to continue this job.

---

accordion) o'nights, that's how he got his beer, he never did buy any beer, no, he would lay his hat on the floor, and play a tune, and they'd chuck the pennies in, or whatever, wasn't much, until he got enough for a pint; Red Lion, I never did see him in the Black Boys, never."

And that's how to handle the price of your beer! He was appreciated for his skills in wood, in music, and in choice of lifestyle.

Cyril Bacon "Old Giddybar's one-man business, he was a carpenter, yeah, a very good carpenter; he built all farm gates, ladders, anything he'd do it in wood, queer old boy, but he did his job... he chose to live in the caravan because he had two daughters, you see, well, 'cos they wanted to get married, and so one of them lived in his house. That's what he wanted, he used to sit on the steps and play his hurdy-gurdy, yes, he loved it..."

But is this really the best way to handle old ladies?

Henry Varden Giddybar Temple - He was quite an old character, he was on Gypsy's Corner in his caravan - I think one of the daughters had his house. He was a carpenter, I remember him telling me he got 3d an hour, I think he worked on the Hanworth Estate. He had a bike, he was a bit of an old devil - he'd go up behind these old dears, he had a great old klaxon horn, and that would go Weerrrhhh! It was all mechanically done, he had that on his crossbar. There were some characters in those days, there aren't the people like it now..."

Children just couldn't keep away.

Brenda Durrant "He lived like a gypsy, in the summer, in his caravan; he played his piano-accordion, wear an old neckerchief, didn't he; mum would say, I don't want you to go round his caravan... and where did we go? The boys used to rock his caravan, didn't they - Brian was a beggar for that, he was terrible... and what did Giddybar do to the boys? He had a little handcart that he used to pee in... and if the boys rocked the caravan... he'd chuck it!" *(Accompanied by sound effects of liquid flying through the air!!!)*

Traders

Fisher's General Store

Both Geoffrey Fisher and his shop (which he ran with his wife Joan) were village institutions for forty years between 1947 and 1987. The business he took over from Jimmy Colman traded primarily in watches and cycles, although petrol had been sold for a while too. Geoffrey quickly turned it into a General Store, continuing with the bikes, and adding fish and chips and wedding photography to his range of services - a miniature hypermarket! The zeal he brought to running the shop was evident too in his lifelong work in public affairs - in particular the communities of Aldborough and Thurgarton, where he was Chairman of the Parish Council for thirty-three years. He was in addition a councillor with the

then Erpingham Rural District Council, the predecessor to the North Norfolk District Council. In these two public roles he worked tirelessly to improve both services and amenities for people in the area. We'll start with a few eyewitness accounts of the shop.

Joan Fisher "We did literally sell everything, we really did - fireworks, fireworks time, toys at Christmas…"

David Cooke "Geoffrey would have so many irons in the fire, he would sell his petrol, he would sell all the brown goods, the radios, all this equipment, watches and all the groceries, you could get everything from there, Christmas goods, if somebody asked him to get something in for Christmas, he'd get it, toys, seeds - the main reason for his success in running a village shop."

Daphne Nichols worked for him from an early age.

Daphne "I used to work for him. I wouldn't go back to school, so father said, you can go and work there; he was quite a fair boss while I was in there; I always worked hard anyway, that was me, but I never found fault with him; the only thing I didn't like was put the wind in the tyres, I thought they were going to blow up! But he was always fair."

He was quick to exploit a new commercial trend.

Joan Fisher "He went in for Walls ice cream, the big van pulled up on the Green, there were so many people waiting, word had got round, he had to shut the shop door and get the ice cream into the fridge at the back via the side door *(chuckles)*. That was the first time there'd been ice cream in Aldborough! They all wanted it… you see, you bought all these things direct, like Crawford's biscuits, sweets, you had all these reps coming in, and it was all direct. Now you couldn't always get a direct account, it took a little bit of getting, and the fact that he got Walls direct was out of this world at the time…"

Daphne Nichols has good reason to remember the ice cream.

Daphne Nichols "It was very hot one Sunday afternoon when they were playing cricket, and he opened the shop just to sell ice creams… I ate ten threepenny Walls bricks… and I wasn't ill afterwards!"

As for his work in the public arena, Geoffrey Fisher was known as a person who made things happen.

Billy Hammond "On arrival, he soon took up work for the village; he became a Rural Erpingham District Councillor for the Aldborough area and Gresham. I think it was from my father that he became Chairman of the Parish Council, which he held for thirty-plus years. Fisher was, so to speak, all get up and go; he got the village its sewer system, then got mains water throughout the village; did much to forward connections to outlying villages and dwellings. Through him, second-hand kerbs were obtained to start the kerbing of the Green. Geoffrey gave time and effort non-stop to get the Community Centre up and running."

However, he would sometimes tread on people's toes - or worse.

Daphne Nichols "He would bulldoze his way through things, he was that kind of a person, not worrying if he did hurt somebody."

More than one sort of bull-dozing was necessary when creating the sewerage system.

Daphne Nichols "Father fell out with him over the sewer, that was put down on one of our meadows... anyway, I suppose if the Council want anything, they have it, don't they? But they fell in again!"

One of his long-term achievements was his campaign to bring Council housing to the village, with beneficial consequences both to local trade and the village school.

Ruth Bayes "He was certainly instrumental in keeping the numbers in the school up as a result of the building of Margaret Lilly Way and Tinkers Close."

Perhaps these comments from David Cooke provide an overview of his work in public affairs.

David Cooke "Undoubtedly, he attracted controversy, but the bottom line is he was fully committed."

The occasion is unknown, but must pre-date the demolition of the old Days' shop, seen in the background. We do know, however, the names of many of the contestants lining up for the race, which must have been billed as the Sisters' Race! Pairs of sisters include;
Audrey and Ruth Chapman,
Cynthia Greene and Muriel Hall (née Colman),
Ruth and Betty Shemming.
It also includes Stella Mason.

Days' Stores

The exterior of the original Days' shop remained substantially unaltered until the mid-fifties, when it was replaced by the large store we know today. John Brown approved:

John Brown Messrs B. G. Day and Sons have demolished their old shop and built a new store on the site, making a great improvement to the appearance of the Green.

For more than twenty years, the shop was run very successfully by Mrs Joyce Day.

The Days' main business was the grocery store, which was run by Mrs Joyce Day; there were also a grocery round and coal deliveries - not to mention a coach, fondly known as Red Rover. There was a coalyard, warehousing and a large orchard at the back of the shop. The grocery round delivered to an area of 60 square miles, making over 80 calls a day when busy. Villages covered included Matlaske, Plumstead, Little Barningham, Wickmere, Erpingham, Calthorpe, Sustead, Gresham, Metton, Antingham, Suffield and Thorpe Market.

A.G. Davison & Son

The photo shows Derrick Davison, Arthur Cole and Herbert Knights.

Here is a snippet from the Eastern Daily Press, November 1955.

Aldborough Post Office has been moved to the shop of Mr D. Davison, after having been about 80 years in the hands of one family. Mr W. Chestney took over the Post Office in the 1870s, and at his death 34 years ago his daughter and son-in-law Mr and Mrs Chapman took charge. Now Mr and Mrs Chapman have retired.

The Post Office business was added to the cobbler's shop, and a family house for the Davisons at the same time. The sorting office was located in a shed behind the house.

Elsie Davison "There were three of us who put in for it - we were fortunate to get it. We were there twenty-eight years, working together, oh yes, definitely, working together."

Barclays Bank

John Brown The opening of a one-day bank in the village took place in 1893.

We know from photographic evidence that early in the century Barclays Bank was based for a while in John Brown's House. Later, it was housed in one of the front rooms of the house that formed part of the Temperance Hall. David Cooke recalls the building.

Mid-century view across the Green from the Black Boys

David Cooke "Facing the front of the house, Barclays Bank was on the left, and there was a lounge to the right; but between the two, there was just an entrance hall or corridor - it was no more than that. And I can see now Leslie and Wilfred Kent, Fred Osborne, queuing up, cramped in this corridor, waiting to do their banking, with their old cloth bank bag. They had to wait there; each customer was served individually, it was a question of confidentiality."

Jean Price worked on the other side of the Green at this time.

Jean Price "I worked at Massingham's, at the desk, from 1966 to 1973. Thursdays was bank day, we were very busy then, because people would come in and buy meat as well."

Elsie Davison "Everybody went into the bank, you saw everybody down there."

Brenda Durrant "I used to love going down there, I felt ever so proud if Dad let me go to the bank! *(laughter)* I was only little!"

Ruth Lambert "That was there when we got married (1964), we opened our account there; everybody used to go down there on a Thursday morning, that was quite a hive of activity; there was no security - they just came in a car - there would be all Kents' takings for the week, Days', the butchers, the two bakeries, the farmers, they must have had quite a lot of money going back to Aylsham, with no security whatsoever - which is why they had to stop, it certainly wasn't through lack of custom."

Kents' Stores

Throughout the period, the shop flourished as a number of businesses under the two Kent brothers, Leslie and Wilfred, later to be joined by Brian Kent. In addition to the general store, they offered a taxi and coach service, providing transport for the older children to their secondary schools. At one time they had as many as five coaches. Alan and Marion Wright remember them as drivers.

Marion Wright "He'd call us, 'You snotty kids!' He'd come flying on the bus if there was anything wrong, and tell us all off. This was Leslie, we called him Tibbo; Wilfred was different altogether."

Alan Wright "Children would be turned off the bus if they misbehaved. Wherever we might be, he'd stop and shout 'Get out!' And they did."

The Kents' business was sold to Gerald Round in October 1972.

Bone & Co

Notes The shop continued trading with Mr Albert Tash as manager, although ownership, originally in the hands of Mary Bone, transferred to Mrs Wilkin, who sold on to Copemans, a grocery wholesaler. They in turn sold it to a syndicate including Albert Tash and the Kent brothers. It eventually closed in 1971.

The Tash family and assistants

In the fifties, in the weeks running up to Christmas, it had a special place in the hopes of Aldborough's children. About three weeks beforehand, the staff would pull down the blinds on the window to the right of the front door. Word would go round, 'Mrs Tash has got the blinds down!' and every day they would rush back from school to see if the blinds were up. Finally, the news came, 'Mrs Tash has got the blinds up!' The children would rush to the shop window to see what toys and games there were for Christmas. Each day they would look to see what had been sold. Who had got the doll? Who had got the snakes and ladders?

To the left of the shop there was a separate building that housed clothing, wallpaper and house mats. When the shop closed, that was moved to the back garden of 'Apple Cottage', where it is to be seen today.

Footnote On retirement, Mr and Mrs Tash moved to number three of the row of cottages beside the shop. Mrs Tash named her house 'Thisledome', which people pronounced 'Thistle dome'. But she meant 'This'll do me'!

Engineering works

A. Wright & Sons

As we already know, the garage was set up in 1936 by Oliver Cooke, who subsequently developed a tractor business on the adjoining land. In 1957, he sold the car side to Arthur Wright, who had worked for him a few years previously. In the intervening years, however, Arthur had set up on his own in Thurgarton, (on the land where his son currently has the pig farm). When he transferred this business to Aldborough, he brought the petrol tanks with him, and one of them is still in use. Originally, the garage had a canopy and a kiosk, but they have both since been removed. Harry Varden was employed as a mechanic for many years, as was John Bishop. Alan and Marion Wright have a ledger of car sales as from 1959, the first being a VW Beetle to Dr Eddy. The names read like a cast list of Aldborough people who have featured in this book! Oh, and the till currently in use was inherited from Oliver Cooke!

Oliver H. Cooke & Son

Oliver Cooke's stand at the first Royal Norfolk Show, Sandringham in 1950 illustrates his move from cycles into agricultural machinery.

The original mill house has now been completely absorbed by the business. Note that the roofline has been raised. The seed business was based in the wooden buildings to the right of the picture.

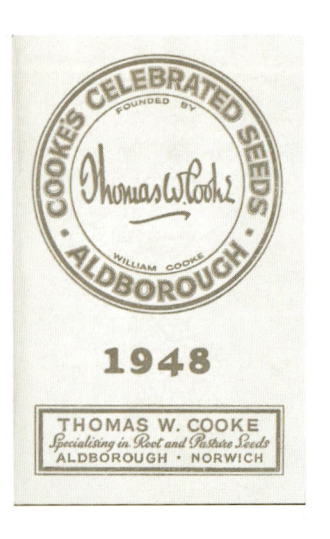

The Mill

David Cooke "In 1955 the mill was very much happening, in full swing, certainly; by that time it had changed from being just a watermill to the installation of what... one, two three very large diesel engines, big single-cylinder Crossley or Ruston and Hornsby engines, I can see them now; even as a younger child I used to love sticking my head through the window and smell the big old diesel engine... And of course the mill by this time was all fitted out with shafting which used to run different kinds of milling machines; there were still, even at that time, the millstones, the original old millstones; they were becoming more and more out of date, of course, but they were still used - if limited use. They were very large, a type of composite granite, seven or eight feet in diameter, very, very heavy. It was mostly hammer mills had been developed then - that was how most of the corn was ground. In earlier years it was mainly flour, but in later years it was much more the different kinds of animal feeds... one particular machine that used to fascinate me was a cattle-cake mill. I don't know what the ingredients were, but it was obviously a meal base, and it also had molasses added to it; but it would come out as a slab of cake; and then another machine would take it and just crumble it up; it had a nice smell to it!

The seed side to the business, agricultural and horticultural; the horticultural seed side was in a separate wooden building, one of the first buildings you came to as you went down Mill Lane; that was under the management of Millie Chapman; I have memories now, as a child, that used to fascinate me, because they had all these lovely coloured envelopes, with flowers on, with vegetables on, they had just about everything. They had these thimble-sized measures, and so they had the bins - I think the seeds must have come in a bin or barrel at that time, because they used to carefully measure them out, open the seed packet, tip it in, seal it up. I've seen as many as, oh, three or four staff in that one office. But... things became redundant, it was no longer viable; what interests remained transferred to Coltishall, where Thomas W. Cooke continued for several years."

Tom Cooke
'Glad to meet you!'

Henry Varden was privy to all kinds of secrets in the lives of the brothers Cooke.

Henry Varden "Tom and Oliver both went to Birmingham, and going along they felt they needed to relieve themselves; so they went over the corner of a field, and Tom commented to his brother that was a wonderful field of mangels; the old boy who owned the field saw them, and came over, and Tom said to him, "You've got some wonderful mangel here, Master!" 'That I have,' he say, 'I get them off Tom Cooke, at Aldborough in Norfolk.' And Tom said, 'I am the man!'"

The introduction to the 1948 seed catalogue presents the Thomas Cooke manifesto in a forthright manner.

Every effort must be made to make the fertile lands of Britain far more productive than they have ever been before. This can be accomplished only with brains, brawn and better machinery. To the task, then - and more - for there is also a Spiritual issue at stake. Unless Britain repents of her Godlessness, we shall find ourselves up against Providence. For 'Man shall not live by bread alone…' It may seem strange to some, that I should, year by year, endeavour to advance the Cause of the Gospel of our Lord Jesus Christ, in the preface of an agricultural seed list, but I am deeply conscious that things Celestial and things terrestrial are indissolubly linked. Our daily bread, therefore, depends also on the goodness of God, Who can give, and Who can withhold, and without Whose beneficent Hand, human prowess counts for nothing.

He was equally straightforward on a one-to-one basis. Lord Walpole was a customer, who was greeted thus.

Tom Cooke "Hallo Walpole, I won't call you Lord, because there is only one Lord."

Other titles were banned, too.

Gwen Coghlan "And he wouldn't call anyone 'Master', either. 'I am the Master', says God. Nor would he allow 'Reverend'"

And in the privacy of his own home he went even further.

Margaret Tidy "I grew up learning that all parsons wore skirts and were wicked. The parson in Aldborough was very High Church, Mr Lilly, he used to pray for the dead, which Dad very much frowned on."

On the product side Thomas Cooke continued to experiment. He continued to test his own seeds and blend his own flour.

Margaret Tidy "He was much more keen on experimenting than on accounts, to be quite honest."

Gwen Coghlan "Nobody would know what was in his concoctions, either; he'd let you have a smell, then you'd have to guess, 'What's in there, my dear?'"

Later, he moved into spices and aromatics.

Margaret Tidy "He had a little book he kept all his recipes in, and the place used to stink often."

Valentine's Day

In the course of our researches, we came across something completely unexpected, even though the WI History does make a brief mention.

WI History St Valentine's Day. On February 14th the children of Aldborough go round from house to house, singing the following verse:

> Good morrow, Valentine,
> God bless the baker
> You'll be the giver,
> I'll be the taker.
> Please, sir, please, sir,
> Will you be so kind,
> To give me something for a Valentine.

The singing custom was well established in the region during the eighteenth century. James Woodforde, the Norfolk parson, recorded his valentine gifts over many years.

Good morrow to your valentine;
Curl your locks as I do mine,
Good morning to your valentine.
I only come but once a year,
Pray give me some money as I stand here,
A piece of cake or a glass of wine,
Good morning to your valentine.

We may read more of this fascinating regional custom in **Where Beards Wag All**, *by George Ewart Evans. Talking of elements of folklore peculiar to East Anglia, George Evans mentions the 'children's custom of visiting the parish priest on Valentine's Day and singing him a traditional Valentine song.' The version he quotes (left) is a version recorded in Essex at the end of the last century.*

George Evans goes on to say, in addition, that 'apparently it was the custom in East Anglia on this day to leave small presents on someone's doorstep, to ring the bell violently and then run away'.

Here are some accounts of the Aldborough variant of this ancient custom still practised in the late forties. First the singing.

Daphne Nichols "Straight from school we would start, only calling at the houses where we knew we would get something. Twenty to thirty of us, we would call at Thurgarton Lodge, Chestnut Farm, all the shops around the Green, Spurgeon's farm, Dr Eddy's, Mrs Gay - she lived across the meadow at Wickmere - and then down to the Revd C. Lilly at Aldborough Hall.

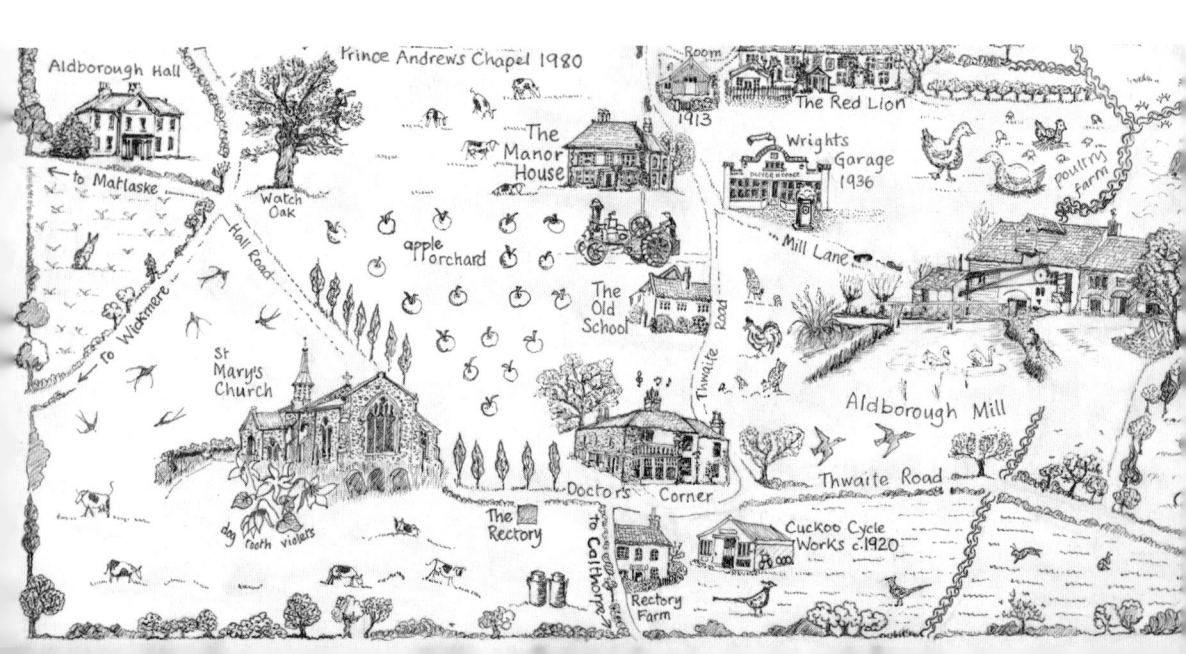

We walked miles across the muddy fields, February, we didn't seem to care, we would sing our hearts out, often repeating songs over and over again. Dr Eddy was always a bit disgusted because we'd sing 'Good Morrow, Valentine' and then we'd go into 'Early one morning' which is a classical piece, he thought that wasn't very good, you know! We used to sing all sorts of songs, anything that we knew at school... The youngest of us would probably be about nine - this would be after the war, obviously, I was seven when the war finished. We'd have the Martins family, there would be Little Titch, I suppose, Sylvia and Delma, two of the girls, they would struggle, Sylvia had bad feet and they would struggle over the fields, and we'd have to keep waiting for them to catch up; and sometimes it would be raining, but we'd still go. We never bothered about our tea until we got home; we'd share the money out at the end; and we also got apples and tangerines and sweets and chewing-gum which we would eat on the way. We'd take shortcuts across fields, and it would be very muddy going across to Mrs Gay's. We were pretty muddy by the time we got home."

Phyllis Whitney "We used to go round singing, too, to the houses; we'd sing 'Good Morrow, Valentine, God Bless the Baker, If you'll be the Giver, I'll be the Taker. Please man, please man, would you be so kind, To give us something for our Valentine.' And we were rewarded! Other than money, the first house was Gay's, right across the fields by Aldborough Church. We had a cake there, there was always a tray of cakes ready; then you'd go to Aldborough Hall, where you'd have a drink as well, I think; you'd come back to Mrs Hammond's, you're all in the kitchen round the table, she had all the money, and she shared it out between us. There was a good few of us who went, it was quite a trek, in the evening, in the dark, no adults, just children."

And now the second aspect - the violent ring of the doorbell.

Elsie Davison "We used to do a parcel up, put a string on it, and I used to go upstairs, or my husband did, into the toilet, stand on the toilet seat, and hang out the window over the back door, you see; then somebody used to knock at the back door, and they used to go and get the parcel - but before they could get the parcel, the string was gone, it was all gone again - that was Valentine; we used to do it two or three times, we give in at the end, I can't quite remember the end."

Brenda Durrant "We used to go to Ruth and Pam's, and knock on the door, and run away, and play all sorts of tricks on people."

Elsie Davison "Gwen Baldwin used to come to you, too, when you got older…"

Brenda Durrant "We played tricks on people…"

Ruth Lambert "We used also to get lots of presents, we used to get colouring books and pens and sweets and apples, all in parcels that were left - you'd get the one that was taken on the string, but a lot of things were left…

Brenda Durrant "You used to get ever so scared, didn't you, as children, it would be dark…"

Ruth Lambert "We still do it, and my son and daughter do it for their children - their respective husband and wife think they're absolutely bonkers.."

The Reverend Christopher Lilly (above with grandchild) retired in 1946.

1946 Aldborough joined with Thurgarton.
1946 Revd T. Beattie
1949 Revd K. Warner
1961 Aldborough and Thurgarton joined with Hanworth and Gunton to form a group of four parishes.
1962 Revd A. Chataway
1966 Revd F. Irwin

A Youth Club dinner with The Revd K. Warner seated far right.

Places of worship

Many of the following comments are taken from a discussion held in the Church Room on the topic of church and chapel. In the early fifties some of the young people liked to sample the full range of denominations available.

Ruth Lambert "They'd finished with the afternoon Sunday School at St Mary's by the time I went; they had the morning one at quarter to ten, the chapel one at half past ten, followed by the Gospel Hall at half past two; I used to do that every Sunday. Six of us, perhaps, did that."

We have space to feature just two individuals from this period - one clergyman and one parishioner. The Revd Keith Warner is well remembered; he worked and played with all sections of the community.

Ruth Lambert "Reverend Warner used to have the Youth Club at his house, quizzes, music and things."

He was a keen cricketer and you should be able to spot him in the team photograph on page 120.

Billy Hammond "He came straight away and played cricket; later on he umpired. That was the usual thing for him to say, when we parted on Saturday evening from the Red Lion, 'Right, chaps, see you in the morning!'"

He didn't favour one pub over the other.

Daphne "Reverend Warner took us carol-singing; we used to end up at the Black Boys; when we'd get there, we'd sing outside, and he had to go in and have a pint - at their invitation, not his!"

And his timing was impeccable.

Ruth Lambert "He used to deliver the Parish magazine, as well, on Saturday mornings; he came just as my mother was getting shortcakes out of the oven!"

He had to learn to take a joke.

Ron Dobbie "And another thing, when PC John Lock and the Reverend Warner used to play, somebody tied a rope to the Rector's bike and put it over the branch of that tree, and pulled it up... *(too much laughter to hear end of story)*."

When he moved on, he was much missed.

Daphne "He was lovely, though, it was a shame when he left, he was liked by the majority of the people, I think."

Eileen Hammond

The notes below were taken from the moving tribute to his mother by her son Billy on the occasion of her memorial service following her death early in 2002.

Notes Susannah Eileen Hammond born a Plumbly at Thurgarton Hall in 1905. She worked with livestock at Villa Farm, Thurgarton before moving to Chestnut Farm on marriage to Burrell Hammond in 1925. Two children were born to them, Billy (in 1926) and sister Anne (in 1929). During the war she was District Organiser for Women's Land Army 1940-46. Throughout her long life, she played an enormous part in the community, in many different roles. She was a member of the Parish Council, a tireless worker for the church, and a member of Aldborough PCC. She was the longest-serving member of Aldborough and Thurgarton WI, and probably the longest-ever member of the WI in Norfolk; this spanned a period of 83 years, having accompanied her mother to the first meeting called by Lady Suffield in 1919; in all this time she was secretary for 20 years and president for 12 years; she was a founder and committee member of the Over 60s club. She cycled everywhere for years, but in 1955 she suffered an accident in the Church Room, which made cycling difficult, so she took up driving. She always loved gardening, but in 1998 she suffered a bad fall. She died in January 2002.

Eileen Hammond, president of the [WI], pictured with her great-grandchildren.

As a one time neighbour, Tony Barber was particularly appreciative.

Tony Barber "But Mrs Hammond did so much by way of help for the village - quite frankly, I cannot understand why she never received a national award, I think she ought to have done. She didn't want publicity and so on, but she did all the cooking for every function that was in the village, right up to the time when she got beyond being on her own, absolutely fantastic she was."

Now some individual recollections taken mainly from that discussion held in the Church Room on the topic of church and chapel.

Ruth Lambert "I married a man from Thurgarton in 1964. We had our reception in the Church Room for 147 people, hot meal, stage included. Mrs Hammond always used to do the flowers, no matter who got married; for my sister's wedding, a few years after mine, Mrs Hammond told me she'd finished the flowers, and invited me up there to have a look at them. We were walking up the path with my son who was about three at the time; we got as far as the wire-netting door, and he said to Mrs Hammond "Is this where you keep your chickens, then?" - she never forgot it! All four of my grand-children were christened there, as were both my children; my husband served there as a teenager; he went to Thurgarton church throughout his youth…"

Marion Wright "I was married in the church, 1970; I was christened in the chapel, went to Sunday School at the chapel, Aunty Elsie played the organ; my three sons were christened at church, James was married there last year; my sister was married the same year, 1970. I also married a man from Thurgarton, the other side of the stream…"

Ruth Lambert "I moved one way over the stream, and you got yours to move the other way over the stream!"

Joan Fisher "I got married in 1952 at Aldborough church, reception at the Church Room *(chuckles)*, Keith Warner married us; I was picked up at my house at the butcher's, and I rather felt like the Queen as I went along; all the locals were out and waving; everyone knew everyone in those days, now I don't know half Aldborough… we had about sixty guests at the reception; the best man was the local baker, George High, and made a most marvellous wedding cake as a present… I've never seen anything… the icing, the decoration had all little bird-cages all round it."

Elsie Davison "The Methodist chapel wasn't licensed for weddings until 1965, when Brenda got married."

Billy Hammond "The Revd Chataway was here for a few years, it was his famous son who was running at the time - he didn't get the mile record, but he was a very fine runner - he was a contemporary of Dr Roger Bannister; I remember seeing him in the church, the reverend was a bald-headed man, but Christopher had tons of ginger-coloured hair."

Ruth Lambert "The attitude was different at one time, the churches and chapels were a bit anti each other. I went with Mrs Chataway to Buxton vicarage and did a course. I used to do Sunday School there; and then it finished for some reason; some while afterwards, Mrs Impson came to see me about running the chapel Sunday School; I was worried about this - I thought it would be frowned upon - so I went to see the vicar, whoever it was at the

Geoffrey & Joan Fisher cutting their wedding cake in 1952

time, I can't remember - and he said, 'Get it through, my dear, whichever way you do it, get it through.' It was changing by then."

Jean Cooke "I didn't come until 1954, when we had the old Gospel Hall which must have been built at the beginning of the century (1906) - David's parents were the first to be married there, I think. The Sunday School treat was the event of the year for families like the Cookes and the Nicholls from Thurgarton... we used to go and collect them from Sunday School, David and I; David used to dress them, put their shoes on, their socks, get them ready, get them in the mini-bus, take them to Sunday School."

Ruth Lambert "One amusing thing when I took the Sunday School at chapel; when Michael Knights who lived next door, was a tiny little boy, about four, I should think, he came marching into the chapel; I can picture him now, he came in with his little hat on, a German-type hat, he had a feather in. I suppose he'd always been told he lived next door to God's house, so when he came in, he said, 'Well, where is He, then, where is He?'"

Jean Cooke "David was taking Sunday School, and it was Titch Martin, I think, and David was trying to teach them the 'I am's' of Christ; and he wanted them to think of 'I am the light'. So to encourage a reply, David said to them, 'Well, what's coming in through the window?' And the boy said, 'It's a draught, sir'!"

The Church Room was used constantly for wedding receptions, parties, and entertainments of all kinds.

Daphne Nichols "Concert parties were held, performing dogs, magicians; once I was sawn in half - I was petrified; I didn't volunteer, I was pushed up! The mobile cinema was held on Tuesday nights, a full-length film plus one or two others. There were hard forms and chairs to sit on, but you got used to them; there were old-fashioned coal stoves for heat; dances were held quite frequently when I was a teenager, refreshments always provided, sandwiches, cakes, tea and orange."

It doubled as a cinema for a while.

Brenda Durrant "That was Mr and Mrs Bennett, and Mrs Day was the lady who shone the torch, she took the money, and showed you to your seats; and for an extra, I don't know, a penny, you could have a cushion!"

Ray Spinks Who can forget in the fifties the monthly visit of the cinema van, which used to turn up and show movies in the Church Room? This was of course before the mass ownership of TV, and the visit was eagerly awaited, in spite of the frequent breakdowns and rather crackly sound.

Sport

Cricket

Ron Dobbie "I was de-mobbed in 1946, I come down to watch the cricket, had a little rest, and joined the club in 1947. I attended the AGM in 1949, where I was cajoled into succeeding Mr William Carter the village schoolmaster, who had done the secretaryship for 21 years, as I was the only one in the club who could write! So I've been secretary/treasurer ever since! And Mr Carter had taken over in the twenties from the previous headmaster, Joe Hulls."

By my reckoning that's just 3 secretaries since 1887 when we read of a young Joe Hulls in the post - a total of 115 years not out! A world record?

Ron Dobbie "I used to come down and watch the cricket before the war, I lived over the border then, I was living up White House then, where my father was Head Gardener. I used to lie in the long grass on the boundary; the Green was very rough and uneven, and if you got 50, that was a winning score! I've known a batsman to hit the ball about 20 yards from the bat, the fielder put his foot on the ball, and when they were in between the wickets, they'd be run out... I carried on playing into my seventies, eight or nine years ago. In my career, I've taken over three and a half thousand wickets, I've taken 100 wickets a season 14 times, my highest score was 29 not out..."

Ron Dobbie contributes a brief summary of the club's post-war history.

Ron Dobbie The club participated in the now defunct North Norfolk League before the Second World War, and up to the 1950s. In the early 1950s they won the North Norfolk Shield and Rothermere Cup, both under the captaincy of Reg Hunn.

Ron Dobbie

Team photograph 1950

Back row: David Gee (boy), Geoff Martins, John Mason, Michael Allen, Wilfred Bishop, Norman Reynolds, Geoff Cussey, Arthur Godley.

Front row: Revd K. Warner, Robin Creasey, Reg Hunn (Capt.), Tom Gee, Ron Dobbie.

Over more than fifty years Ron Dobbie has grown to be the very backbone of Aldborough Cricket Club, apart from his other roles as major wicket-taker, heroic number 11 batsman, secretary, umpire, club historian and groundsman.

Two England Test players have played at different times on Aldborough Green, Clive Radley (Surrey and England) and Peter Parfitt (Fakenham Grammar School, Middlesex and England). A.J. Parfitt brought his eleven, which included his son Peter, on 29 June 1957. He was bowled by Reg Hunn for 25.

Reg Hunn captained the team from 1946-60, and served the club for 64 years until his death in 1999.

Football

Notes The club was re-formed after the war, in 1946, with Mr L. Shaw as secretary. Home games were played on a piece of land belonging to Mr Billy Hammond behind the old Post Office. At different times teams played in the Reepham League and the Holt and District League, enjoying considerable success in local Cup competitions. They moved to the Green in the early 1950s when the surface was levelled. The club disbanded in 1958, to be re-formed in 1962 with Mr Bob Bishop as secretary, a position he still holds. We joined the North East Norfolk Football League on its inception, and over the years have won both Division 3 and Division 2 titles. During this period the club also won the Cromer Lifeboat Cup.

Team photograph 1948

Back row from left
Alfred Morgan, Henry Wells, Freddie Pike, ? Shaw, John Gray, Ernie Pike, ? Goodson, Russell Lee

Front from left
Bertie Cook, Alan Keeler, Dessie Mallett, John Drury, Reg Hunn

Team photograph

Back left to right
Mrs Eddy, Edna Newstead, Mrs Warner, Marjorie Day, Phyllis Morgan, Mrs Crame

Front left to right
Mrs Norman, Joan Fisher, Mrs Reynolds, Jean Price, Doris Moll

Ladies football

Joan Fisher "I do remember the highlight of our football was when the Norwich City footballers came and played. That was when we were raising money to get the Green correct; there was a dance in the Church Room in the evening, that was one of the highlights of my early youth, it really was good; there were more supporters round the Green than the men used to get; that was great fun; it would have been 1952 or 1953."

Boxing

Dick Price started boxing as a teenager; he was trained by Jack Dennis, himself a former professional boxer who lived at Tweenways in Thurgarton. He formed a club which trained in the upstairs backroom of the Black Boys. Through Jack's connections other professional boxers were invited to exhibition bouts in the village. Dick continued boxing while doing his National Service and continued as a boxing coach later in life.

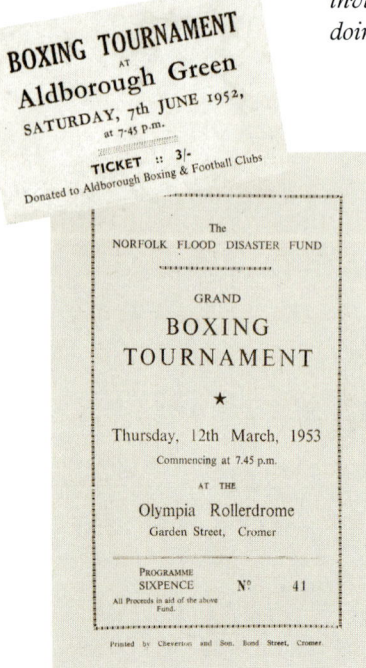

BOXING TOURNAMENT
AT
Aldborough Green
SATURDAY, 7th JUNE 1952,
at 7.45 p.m.
TICKET :: 3/-
Donated to Aldborough Boxing & Football Clubs

The
NORFOLK FLOOD DISASTER FUND

GRAND
BOXING TOURNAMENT
★
Thursday, 12th March, 1953
Commencing at 7.45 p.m.
AT THE
Olympia Rollerdrome
Garden Street, Cromer

PROGRAMME
SIXPENCE   N° 41
All Proceeds in aid of the above Fund.

Printed by Cheverton and Son, Bond Street, Cromer.

PROGRAMME OF EVENTS

Junior Contest		Three Two-Minute Rounds	Junior Contest		Three Two-Minute Rounds
A. YOUNG Buxton A.B.C.	v	**E. COLMAN** Buxton A.B.C.	**J. DAVIS** Buxton A.B.C.	v	**R. BUSH** Buxton A.B.C.
Junior Contest		Three Two-Minute Rounds	Junior Contest		Three Two-Minute Rounds
N. CULLEY Aldborough A.B.C.	v	**G. HOUGHTON** Buxton A.B.C.	**D. BUCKFIELD** Buxton A.B.C.	v	**L. SMITH** Aldborough A.B.C.
Bantamweight Contest		Three Two-Minute Rounds	Welterweight Contest		Three Two-Minute Rounds
DICK PRICE Aldborough A.B.C.	v	**L. CASH** R.E.M.E.	**B. GOLDWATER** R.E.M.E.	v	**A/c. J. HILL** R.A.F.
L/Heavyweight Contest		Three Two-Minute Rounds	L/Heavyweight Contest		Three Two-Minute Rounds
G. MUDD R.E.M.E.	v	**Cpl. WHITE** R.A.F.	**K. KYNMAN** R.E.M.E.	v	**A/c. D. HENNESY** R.A.F.
Welterweight Contest		Three Two-Minute Rounds	L/Middleweight Contest		Three Two-Minute Rounds
J. WOODCOCK Aldborough A.B.C.	v	**J. WILLIAMS** Norwich A.B.C.	**R. BALLANTINE** R.E.M.E.	v	**G. BISHOP** Norwich A.B.C.
Lightweight Contest		Three Two-Minute Rounds			
D. McNALLY R.E.M.E.	v	**A/c. FOX** R.A.F.			
Flyweight Contest		Three Two-Minute Rounds	Lightweight Contest		Three Two-Minute Rounds
C. MARSHALL Norwich A.B.C.	v	**K. AMIS** Aldborough A.B.C.	**G. WHITE** R.E.M.E.	v	**A/c. G. MURPHY** R.A.F.

INTERVAL OF 15 MINUTES

The School

Mr Carter continued as Headmaster until his retirement in 1950, after twenty-five years in the post. He was succeeded by Mr Stanley Crame, who had started his career in teaching as a pupil-teacher, shortly before his fourteenth birthday, at Aylsham Boys' School.

Mr Crame, Mr Featherstone, Mr Jones, Mr Laborde. Mrs Hall, Ida Impson, Mrs Rook, Miss Bee.

The school log for 1953 records the following sad news.

June 1, 1953 Mrs M. Lilly of Aldborough Hall died this morning. This lady had for many years taken a great interest in the school, as a school manager and friend.

However, John Brown records that later in the year 'extensions to the school building were carried out with a view to this becoming a central school; this scheme was afterwards altered on the building of Aylsham Secondary Modern School.' The new wing was used for the first time on September 9 1953.

A list of those present at this discussion:

Ruth Lambert, (née Daniels) 1948-54
Phyllis Whitney (née Barker) 1943-51
Elsie Davison (née Hunn) 1923-37
Brenda Durrant (née Davison) 1951-57
Maureen Bane (née Grey) 1953-58
Shirley Wright (née Grey)
Janice Single (née Kent)

Preparations for this book included a School Reminiscence evening, chaired by Penny Jackson, where a few past pupils (all female, as it happened!) recalled their schooldays. Comments about the school ranged from the twenties to the sixties, but I have tried to record them here in a reasonably chronological order. We start with a few random observations. There was much laughter!

Elsie Davison "Mr Hulls was the Headmaster then, then Mr Wheeler came, then Mr Carter came, so we always used to say, we've had the halter, we've had the wheels, and we had the cart, we always used to laugh and say that."

Was selection for transfer to Grammar School strictly on merit?

Elsie Davison "When I went to school, there was only two passed *(to grammar school)* in the whole school, and there was only one could go… don't know why, but we always said, the Headmaster's

123

Ida Impson

Ida Impson, daughter to Robert Massingham, carrier, worked as school secretary for many years. As you will have read, she was a wonderful source for much of the material for the early years of this book. Born in 1906, she spoke to me in 2001 of the outbreak of the First World War, a length of time ago which seemed impossibly long. Her husband Ernie took over the carrier's business from her father, and continued until the early 50s. They lived in Olden Cottage just this side of the beck, and many Aldborough people have a strangely fond memory of wet weather in their schooldays: when the water got too deep, Ernie would put on his waders and carry them across the stream! Ida was a devout Methodist all her life, a respected local preacher who passed her exams by correspondence. She had a warm and welcoming presence, and was devoted to the village where she lived for over 93 of her 96 years.

daughter was one, and my brother Reg *(Hunn)* was the other, and you know who went through, don't you…"

Marion "I remember Dad *(Reg)* saying that he and his mum biked to North Walsham for an interview, and he always thought he wasn't chosen because the family couldn't afford to buy the uniform."

Strikes with the arm were part of the teacher's daily repertoire.

Group "Mr Hulls was the strict one, Mr Carter was the one who used the cane, I can see him getting it out of the bottom drawer in his desk, out it'd come… and Mr Crame had big hands, huge hands, which he'd use, oh, he'd use them."

Brenda Durrant "When Peter was a little boy, he was playing with a friend who had thrown a piece of wood with a nail in it and gashed his head all open, so Dr Eddy in those days used to stitch them up, so he went into school the next day with a letter saying, do not let anybody touch Peter's head with this great big bandage on… well, he was naughty in class, and his Infant teacher got a big book and whammed him on top of the head… so back to the doctor he went…"

Ruth Lambert "Mr Crame terrified me so much that I used to shake when I had to go to Parents' Evenings, honestly…"

The school's emphasis on Rural Studies led to enthusiastic experiments with the effects of stinging nettles on rarely-exposed flesh.

Group "The toilets were down the bottom there, and they weren't flush ones, and there was a space under the door, and the boys used to…" (story involves the words 'boys' 'poking under the door' 'stinging nettles' and mimes for their intended destination and hoots of giggles!!!!)

Some teachers are remembered with affection.

Brenda Durrant "Mr Featherstone was lovely, wasn't he…"

While others inscribe themselves into memory for different reasons.

Brenda Durrant "On her blackboard, Mrs Hall had 'Good, better, best, never let it rest/ Until your 'good' is better, and your 'better' best.' Now why do I remember that? Perhaps we had to chant it…"

The playground had its own revenge chant.

Group "'Old Ma Hall is a rum old geezer, she's got a face like a lemon-squeezer' - she went on for ever. And…we used to knit dishcloths, hundreds and hundreds of dishcloths, and socks, we did proper dish-cloth stitch, didn't we Maureen, this old white thick wool. I made a pillow-case with Mrs Hall, with draw-threads."

In April, 1956 the school received a visit from Daniel Akinlade Adejumo, a student-teacher from Western Nigeria. He spent a fortnight in the school as part of his year's training with the London Institute of Education.

He made a big impression on the Aldborough children.

Group "Do you remember Mr Adejumo? He was a Nigerian, wasn't he, he was the first coloured person we'd ever seen, he just came to our school, to visit; he stayed with Mr Crame, didn't he; he could walk across the playground on his hands; he was probably a student-teacher; there wasn't really any explanation of who he was or where he was from, he seemed so different; he was very nice, once you got to know him."

Mr Crame demonstrates the arts of bee-keeping to pupils and Mr Adejumo

Marion Wright *"Every year we had to draw the head, the thorax and the body."*

The character of the school changed fundamentally when Aylsham Secondary Modern School opened in September 1957.

Inspection, June 1957 This is a good rural school, giving the children a sound training and a good general education, much of it through the work in Rural Studies. The garden which is the centre of much of this work is not only well-kept and well-used, but also forms a pleasing setting for the school. This term 199 children aged 5 to 15 are attending the school; most of them entered as Infants and have worked their way up the school. The others, about ten in number, each year are transferred to this school at the age of 11, from Matlaske and Wickmere. It is with genuine regret that at the end of this term, this school will lose its seniors.

But it has to be said that was only one side of things.

Group "Gardening - one year they trashed all the gardens, the cane did come out; there used to be four squares, as you walk out to the playing-field, they each had a section; one year they had a riot and everything got trashed... I know the year that *(name withheld)* left school, they broke the cane, and put it back in his cupboard; and the next year when they got the cane out, Mr Crame had to hold it in the middle, because it was broken... poor little John was going to get the cane, but he didn't get it because it was broken!"

In December 1960 Wickmere School closed, with the 27 pupils and their teacher, Miss E. Peckham, transferring to Aldborough.

Miss Peckham was born in 1912, and grew up in Itteringham in a cottage belonging to the Wolterton estate. She attended Itteringham village school, trained as a teacher at Keswick Hall in Norwich and spent thirty-eight years teaching in and around Aldborough. She started her career in a small private school for about ten pupils founded by Mrs Hammond.

Miss Peckham "She wanted her children to have private education, so all her friends used to come there. They used to come at age five and went on to boarding-school aged eleven."

However, when the war broke out, such a small school was thought to be a luxury, and as there was a shortage of teachers, Miss Peckham went to Wickmere, where she taught for twenty years. In 1960, Norfolk Education were going to close either Erpingham or Wickmere; they decided on the latter, and all the children had to go to Aldborough; Miss Peckham went too, staying until her retirement twelve years later.

Miss Peckham "That was a very happy twelve years, with the other teachers, Mrs Crouch, Mrs Rook and Mr Crame. He was very strict, but he knew his job and he got down to it; and he was a disciplinarian, he wouldn't have any nonsense at all, because in those days you could use the cane, you see; he didn't use it frequently, he was very good to them, and the boys all liked him. He was good on his job, he knew his work."

But it is in connection with her voluntary work with the Red Cross that Miss Peckham is equally remembered. For over thirty years, from her girlhood in Itteringham through her career as a teacher, she both underwent extensive training as a cadet nurse herself, and in turn led the very strong local branch over a long period.

Ruth Lambert "She used to teach us Red Cross - we went to Carrow Abbey in Norwich, we went in for a competition which we won; we were so pleased - and on the way home we put chocolate buttons all round her hat, poor lady…"

Miss Peckham gave private lessons too. One of her pupils was the young Lord Walpole.

Lord Walpole *"Miss Ivens never taught us money; whether she didn't like money, whether she thought it was vulgar, we never learnt to add up pounds shillings and pence; of course this was fairly necessary to get into a prep school. Miss Peckham came over here on many occasions, in fact we went up to the nursery, which was in the wing and we did pounds shillings and pence; to the right effect, because I got into Maple Hall, mainly due to her I suspect."*

Before family ownership of a private car became the norm, medical services were offered through the school.

Elsie "The dentist used to come in the playground with his caravan, Mr Sumpter."

Phyllis "All I can remember is that great big thing he stuck in your mouth, used to go one at a time to get our teeth done; he was a bit rough, wasn't he, no anaesthetic."

Brenda "If you had a tooth out, you used to go and ask Mrs Jordan for a clove, and she used to put this clove in your mouth."

Brenda "We had X-rays, didn't we, we had to take all our clothes off and have our chests examined."

Phyllis "We used to go into the Headmaster's house for medical exams... I had a wonky heart, and they had me jumping up and down on his armchair for so long, then he'd listen again... They didn't do anything about it, I just got out of doing exercises. The same thing happened when I was at Wymondham, it happened again."

Marion "The fair-children used to come into school for the week."

Lord Walpole "It's always very important, Aldborough Fair, it's the date isn't it? 'The sugar beet must be across the rows by the time Aldborough Fair comes on.' Do you know that? The point is, in the days when the beet was hoed and singled by hand, one was always much more conscious of it, and once they grow out and touch across the rows, they suppress the weeds - it's very important they do that by midsummer."

Brenda "May Day we used to have the maypole out on the Green and dance round the maypole, do you remember?"

Phyllis "My uncle set the conker-tree by the gate, his class set the conker to grow that tree."

Penny "And the other one, the pink one, which is by the canteen entrance, was planted by Miss Peckham."

Ruth "Ernie Impson used to carry us through to school with thigh-boots on, carry all the children through to school..."

Brenda "There was no reason you never got to school, because he used to carry you, every child, one by one..."

Group "Night-prayer "Lord keep us safe this night/ Safe from all our fears/May angels guard us while we sleep/Till morning light appears."

Group "I can remember the Saving Stamps on a Monday - sixpence for Princess Anne, and a shilling for Prince Charles - but we aren't quite sure, it might have been half a crown! You used to stick them in a little book, and get a certificate, and then change it at the Post Office."

Group "Miss Bee took us to London Zoo, wearing a dress with bees all over it. she always used to wear that, perhaps it was the only dress she had."

Janice "One year we went to London Airport to see Concorde; I can remember Mr Crame measuring out the length of it on the school field."

Janice "There were some very basic things not taught; punctuation, verbs, encouraged to express oneself, some table-learning with Miss Peckham, but after that, no."

Brenda "To be quite honest, when we were at school, none of the richer people's children were at school with us, were they. None of the farming people, they'd go to Sutherland House in Cromer, or Bracondale in Norwich."

Group "I can remember wearing a liberty bodice - with a camphor bag sewn in it! - and rubber buttons that went through the mangle, all right.. we used to have an onion hanging up in the kitchen to keep the germs out!" *(Hoots of laughter...)*

Maureen "We used to have an afternoon rest, with our heads laid on our arms."

Janice "Mr Crame was very mellow in older age; he'd occasionally lose his temper, so he would get the cane or the slipper, but he was very laid back... he suffered from shell-shock (I was told so, anyway), his hands shook; when he was eating his dinner, that was when you noticed it."

Group "He was very strict on table manners, you always had to eat all the food on your plate, disgusting, beetroot with gravy, lumpy mashed potato - I won't eat mashed potato even now - one dollop it was."

Janice "I tell you a game they used to play - I was reminded of this when we moved here - one of the guys working on our barn was at the school at the same time as I was - and he reminded me. Well, they used to have a party after school, so it was dark when you came out; well, there was a game where Mr Crame and Mrs Crouch would sit, and they were dressed up as the king and queen. They used to leave a space, kind of in-between them, but you wouldn't notice as a child, and they'd choose someone new to the school to come and sit with them; and as the child went to sit down, they both stood up, and the child fell straight down through the gap - there was a blanket over the top. Well, this guy was new, and he said, 'I'll never forget that!' - they did that to him. The rest of us thought it was wonderful! It would be child abuse now, wouldn't it?"

The Painted Doll was put on by Reggie Hunn and Mr and Mrs Marshall in 1953

Hilary Mitchell, Jennifer Shemings, Wendy Butcher, Pauline Arnup, Celia and Caroline Crame, Pam Daniels, Lesley Mitchell, Judith Day, Sandra Butcher, Janet Hunn, Brenda Davison(crouching), Marion Hunn (bride), Peter Davison (groom) and Malcolm Mallett (vicar)

Tony Barber feeding his hens

Tony Barber's Poultry Farm
Outstanding Example of Private Enterprise

So read a headline in The Journal, of June 28 1963, and it concerned the poultry business founded by Tony Barber. You may recall that Tony came to live in Thurgarton in 1939, when his father's business folded due to the outbreak of war. He attended Aldborough Primary School, transferring to Paston Boys' Grammar School at North Walsham at the age of eleven. But Aldborough School's tradition of promoting the study and practice of rural science had already made its mark on Tony; he went on to train and work as a teacher himself, and while still living at his parents' home, he set up in his own business of rearing poultry.

The Journal To develop from a small fold unit with 20 laying pullets in a cottage garden to an intensive 1000-bird unit in six years is in itself an achievement; but add to it the fact that it was brought about by a schoolteacher who had limited capital and then it really measures up to a success story. The man behind this outstanding piece of private enterprise is Mr Anthony Barber, of Old School Cottages, Aldborough, who is head of the Rural Science Department at Cromer Secondary Modern School. Careful book-keeping on the fold unit showed the profit that was to be gained from egg production, and it was decided to expand. With limited space as well as capital, it seemed virtually impossible to increase the number of birds by any large number, but Mr Barber's ingenuity was such that he was able to construct, to his own design, a straw-bale house large enough to house 75 birds for under £5.

The article goes on to outline the stages by which Tony reached the 1000 mark, and compliments him on his refusal to reduce the floor-space allowed to each bird. Tony tells us more about the old school.

Tony Barber "The old school buildings - during the war they were used as a store for wastepaper; all the kids used to go round and collect paper, because it was of national importance. I believe it belonged to the Wilkin family, who lived in the house nearest the road. Osborne bought them, turned them into three cottages, Freddy Norman, who was his senior baker, Craskes were in the cottage in-between, I was there, in the cottage at the end. It's from there that I ran my poultry business opposite."

Over 60s club

Notes The club was founded at the end of 1964, by a group that included Mrs Chamberlain, Mrs Newstead, and Mrs Hammond. The first committee meeting was chaired by Revd A. Chataway, where those already mentioned and the following people were present: Mr A. Colman, his housekeeper, and Mrs Hunn. For the early meetings, cars were used to transport members to Thurgarton Rectory, for games sessions where prizes were offered, and Mrs Hammond baked cakes for all. The club proved quickly to be a success, and transferred its meetings to the Church Room. In addition to the regular meetings, day outings took place in the summer and autumn, and winter activities included a Christmas lunch and evening visits to pantomimes and concerts. When the Revd A. Chataway left the district, his place was taken by the Revd Frank Irwin, and then the Revd Eric Moreton, who for several years hosted an annual garden party in his home, The Crest, Alby Hill. At this time, the chairman was Mrs Stacey. The club is proud to have given parties to honour the 90th birthday for several members; perhaps the most notable was that given for Mr 'Happy' Simmonds, who enjoyed tea at Sheringham station, followed by his first ever trip on a railway! Other 90th birthday parties were given to: Mrs Trease, Mrs Massingham, Mr Gooch and Mrs Impson.

(In 1989, Mrs Chamberlain, who had been involved throughout, retired, and her place was taken by Mrs Connie Harmer, with Mr Gilbert Halliday as Treasurer. The club was invited to Mangay House sheltered accommodation, and continued with its tradition of outings and Christmas lunch. The Millennium was celebrated with a party in the Community Centre with a group of singers providing the entertainment.)

Doctor Talk

For a view of Aldborough life from inside the consulting room, we asked Dr Philip Wood to talk with his predecessor Dr Colin Skipper, who took over from Dr Angwin Eddy in 1973. First, however, we may benefit from some inside knowledge of the real reason for that freezing waiting-room from the eventual purchasers of his house.

Karen Fidgen A thin and ill-fitting door, facing due north, formed the entrance to the waiting-room and was surrounded by a half-inch gap through which the north wind blew. The room was fitted with narrow wooden benches, under which there were three or four three-foot long cylindrical 'pew heaters' which were ostensibly there to provide some heating; however, investigations revealed that on the other side of the wall the wires, very tarnished, stopped, plugless, some feet short of any electrical socket. It seemed they had never been wired into a plug and we concluded that the doctor had been heating the waiting-room entirely by means of the placebo effect!

The doctors' discussions ranged over many aspects of the practice, and one of their conclusions, on reviewing the changes seen ever since the time of Dr Eddy's arrival in 1929, was that more had changed in the last twenty years than the previous fifty. Hearing some of their comments makes it easy to see how! Dr Skipper outlines some of his early discoveries.

Colin Skipper "I asked Angwin if I should have an answering machine; to which he replied, 'Well, I can't see the point, 90% of patients don't have a telephone, and those who do can't use them.'"

Communication at night, too, avoided the necessity of a phone.

Colin Skipper "Angwin had some device in the door whereby

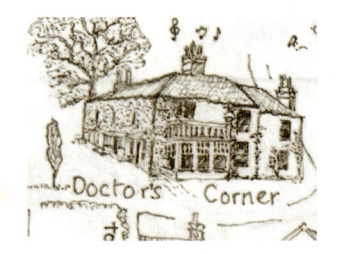

To properly appreciate the following revelation from Joyce Day, we need to understand that both the gentlemen concerned, John Brown and Dr Eddy, were known to be thoroughly tactile chaps.

Joyce Day "As John Brown lay dying, he summoned Dr Eddy for the last time. The doctor told him of his patient's impending exit from this life in as gentle a manner as possible. 'My old friend, I have to tell you that it's a case of… touch and go.' John Brown thought a while before making this reply. 'Doctor, I'm happy about the 'touch', but to be honest, I'm not altogether sure about the 'go'.'"

John Brown died in 1964, at the age of 87

patients could call him in the night, some loudspeaker device, which they shouted through."

He provide some other details of the good doctor's facilities in 1972.

Colin Skipper "He practised in a consulting-room which was an annexe to his dining-room, quite small; there was enough room for a couch and a desk. He didn't even have running water - he had a big enamel jug, but to wash your hands you had to go through to his bathroom. And then a further annexe to the annexe you were already in was the waiting-room. From here, everyone could hear the whole conversation in the consulting-room - the whole village would know before the end of the surgery. The dispensary, very primitive, just a little alcove with a few bottles."

Dr Eddy was sensitive about the demographic range of his patients.

Colin Skipper "There was a tradition in Angwin's day that gentry went to Cromer, or elsewhere, and the farmworkers went to him. He was always disappointed about this, it always upset him; and it was still partly so when I came. And it upset him even more when they couldn't contact their doctor and they came here and consulted him… I'm sure they got very short shrift!"

Dr Skipper talks of some of the aspects to his practice between 1973 and 1992.

Colin Skipper "In the early days either my wife or I answered the phone, I had to get my own records out, see the patient, drive into Aylsham to collect the drugs, then leave them out on a table in the waiting room for the patient to collect - and leave the £1 prescription charge - 95% did! I was on call 24 hours a day, except when I went on holiday and had a locum in. As regards midwifery, I delivered most of the babies myself, either in Longacre, or North Walsham; only abnormal cases would go to Norwich. Simple casualty cases would go to Cromer, otherwise Norwich. There was a large geriatric unit at St Michael's, Aylsham. The list size when I came was about 1100, increasing to 1700 by the time I'd left."

Dr Skipper had previously been practising in Sussex, and was quite taken aback by some of the patients' living conditions he encountered. Some of the more remote cottages had seen little modification in fifty years.

Colin Skipper "A female patient was very ill with cancer; one Friday evening her husband turned up on his bike, saying he thought his wife was dying; so I went there; I knew they didn't have electricity, but there was always an Aladdin lamp there, and I assumed they used it; it wasn't until I got there, and he took me up to the bedroom with a candle, that I realised they didn't! It was the only time I've pronounced anyone dead by candlelight! And it was almost exactly the same when he came to die - except in his case it was torchlight. Again, early in my time here, I had a patient with arthritis. Now the nurse always had to make an appointment to go and see him, and I always wondered why; it wasn't until I went there that I realised that in order for him to have a blanket bath, the wife had to boil up two pans on an Aladdin stove. There was no other means of heating, and the cooking was done in an old tin oven."

Nothing could have prepared him for the ways of this patient.

Colin Skipper "This concerns one of my patients with anaemia; now his nurse never understood why he always had to know the expected time of her arrival and why he always met her at the gate. They had to go into his shed to have the injection. It was only some time later, when the fellow died and the police had to break in, and they found the room was absolutely full of feathers, feathers everywhere, there was nothing else apart from a bed."

And he adds this general comment about housing in the early seventies.

Colin Skipper "Most cottages have now been bought and modernised, but most didn't have running water or loos in the house. I used to be very concerned about the number of cottages becoming holiday houses, and the impact this would have on the practice."

Aldborough Apples

Notes The orchards on the road leading to Matlaske from Doctor's Corner were the enterprise of Major J. J. Barclay. In 1948 he acquired both the Old Rectory and some land bought from Mr Spurgeon. He set about planting apples, setting fives acres in 1949, together with a significant acreage of both celery and runner beans. After a while, he ceased vegetable production, concentrating on the orchards which extended to 30 acres. Varieties included Discovery, Cox's Orange Pippin, Bramley, and Egremont Russet. Overall, the pattern of business could be seen on a five-year cycle, with four years of modest returns, and a fifth of 'good money'. This came about when a frost badly affected orchards in Kent; the site here in Aldborough, however, was generally frost-free, and being near the sea, warmer. The business employed one full-time foreman.

The history of other lands bring unexpected outcomes elsewhere; in the case of British apples, it was the French colonial war in Algeria which brought an adverse consequence to apple-growers here. Following that war, there was a re-settlement programme in France which involved the planting of the Golden Delicious variety. The trees currently in production were planted in 1987.

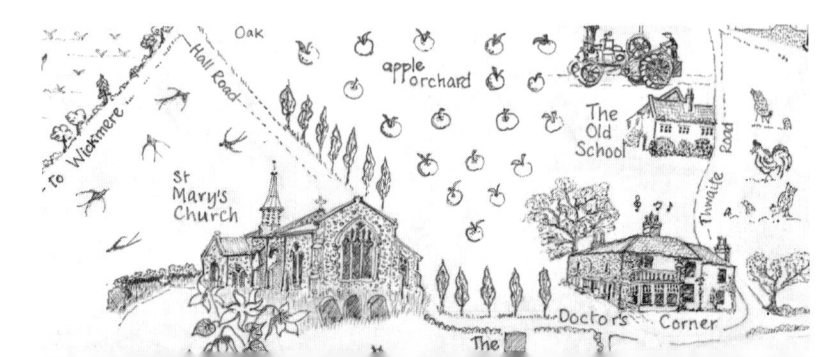

Youth Club

In the late sixties there was a thriving youth club, run by David Cooke and Charles Matts, who dreamed up wild and wonderful activities to entertain the young people. The age range was twelve to nineteen, and at its peak it had fifty members. It offered trips out of the village in the form of special youth camps, to Oulton Broad, for example, but we will focus here on some of the homegrown antics. One of the parents of teenagers involved was Jean Price, reminiscing with David Cooke.

Jean "Well, they used to do such interesting things, they did these wide games, I can remember. My son, who was sixteen at the time, was one of the key members, and Suzy, my daughter, too; they couldn't wait for Friday to get down there."

Temperance Hall before conversion.

David "Yes, your son Christopher was my right-hand man at that time, and one of his ideas was to send out invitations to about ten or twelve other youth clubs - there'd be a hundred or two about. It was late autumn, and Chris designed a skeleton for the old boiler room in the derelict Temperance Hall; he rigged it so that when you opened the door, the cords both activated the skeleton right in the corner, making it rise slowly; and at the same time a light came on, a dim light… this thing rose up as you pushed the door opened!"

Jean "The girls screamed, didn't they? And he did another one, too, in an old barn, and he had a ghost there, a sheet all painted and done, you know; the ghost went up like this and the girls screamed. You had different points where you had to stop and give an answer to get information about where you had to go next."

David "Once we electrified a five-bar gate, too, so they got a shock! But the outstanding one in my memory was when we borrowed an old wrecked car from Arthur Wright's garage, and wheeled it down the road and put it over into Billy Hammond's field; there were still some wheels just on the road, its nose was down in the ditch, and Charles Matts lay there, just outside the driver's seat with tomato ketchup all over him… Well, one of the people living down on the

Green came home that way, jumped out of her car, took one look, dialled 999, oh! The police were soon there, well that was nearly the end of orienteering that night!"

Charles Matts

As we have just seen, Charles Matts helped David Cooke run the Youth Club. He and his wife Marianne arrived in the village in 1966. They had originally met in New Zealand, where Marianne had been brought up, but came to the UK, choosing to settle in Norfolk. Initially, Charles was employed in a joinery business in Aylsham, but when that burnt down, he decided to go solo, working in a lean-to at the side of his house.

Charles Matts "Lo and behold, a council official came along, and said, 'You can't do that sort of thing here!' We were very fed up, but anyway, one Friday evening at Youth Club I was talking to David about this, and he said he had some spare land at the bottom of his workshop I could use. I got planning permission and had a workshop there for nearly ten years. The Cooke influence was crucial, David never wanted anything for it, rent, anything, we were there for the thick end of ten years, actually."

The business prospered, and the time came to buy a property where he could both live and work. Manor Farm Thurgarton came up for auction. He and his wife bought the property, but unknowingly acquired a sitting tenant too.

Charles Matts "There was an old lady living in this place, Mrs Willis-Frances, who was rather an extraordinary lady. I mean she was a real thorn in my side inasmuch as I wanted the building, but at the same time I hugely admired her - she was quite blind; the only facility in this house was one cold water tap, there was a thunder box at the bottom of the garden, and Social Services had put a rope from the back door that she could follow; she was quite a grand lady and incredibly tough; it was perishingly cold in here, she lived with her dog, the state of it was unbelievable."

Charles had now the basis on which to build his business. He converted the barns into a workshop, and after the death of Mrs Willis-Francis, he started to modernise the farmhouse. He took on staff, he diversified from joinery into furniture and he was soon making fine pieces from English hardwoods. Shortly afterwards, Alby Crafts opened, giving him display space in a prestigious Craft Centre on the main A140 route. As a further development, he opened a shop in Holt. He is very keen to acknowledge the decisive input of his late wife Marianne.

Charles Matts "In all of this I should like to emphasise her influence - the business probably wouldn't have existed at all without her."

The success of Charles Matts and his Thurgarton furniture business serves to illustrate a major shift in the economy of rural Norfolk. He arrived at a time when the old patterns of village life, based on farming, had broken down. A consequence was the relatively low price of housing

Marianne Matts was Polynesian by birth, and was brought up in New Zealand from the age of ten.
Charles Matts *"Within a couple of years of settling here, she was President of the WI - a very English sort of thing - somewhat strange for somebody from a Pacific island. She remained President for some years."*

compared to other parts of the country; this proved a significant factor in bringing an influx of newcomers to North Norfolk. Times, they were indeed a'changing.

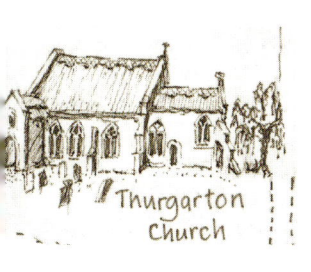

At Thurgarton Church

By George Barker

George Barker was one of the key English poets of the twentieth century, and Thurgarton Church proved a catalyst for this major poetic work which he wrote in 1968. He too was a newcomer to Norfolk, settling with his family in Itteringham, where he lived for many years. (His daughter Raffaella lives and writes in Thurgarton today.) In his wanderings he came upon a large and rather dishevelled church, which set him musing on the universal themes of life and death. The verses printed on the following pages are both stark and beautiful, but repay repeated reading.

Author's notes It is ironic that a building that has for centuries stood as a testament to a living faith should in this poem be the place where the poet finds the 'unspoken No' so powerfully embodied, and here so powerfully expressed. This poem is a beautiful but sombre reflection of the state of 'not having', of 'being without': and its most telling image, the 'masterless dog' makes it reverberate with a sense of loss. The day of the poet's visit has just lost the sun, to be replaced by the 'dead moon'; we read of the 'lost spirit', the 'paralysed stream', the 'dream with nowhere to go'; it is not difficult to find phrases and images shot through with existential despair, written by a man without faith and 'without hope' - but regretfully so: he is painfully aware of what he's missing. And as the church is surrounded by a graveyard where 'Thurgarton's dead lie', so behind all his thinking lurks the prospect of death. Indeed, the very structure of the poem, with the syllable 'oh' chiming at the end of each stanza except the last, brings the toll of the death-knell.

Yet let us think both of the time of this poem's creation, and the particular circumstances of the place. All Saints', Thurgarton is about to be declared redundant, after centuries of being the heart of its community: it truly is a church without a congregation, except the congregation of the dead. Moreover, it stands in a bare landscape where the way of life, based as it has been for centuries on the labour of man and horse, has been eclipsed by the superior efficiency of the machine: beasts are now redundant, leaving the countryside for dead. No wonder it seems the 'barest chapel I know'! But even as death predominates, 'it is from the Tree of Death these leaves of life grow.' And although the dead 'keep here a dark tenancy', they retain 'the right of rising up to go'.

Perhaps, after all, death does not have the final sting.

At Thurgarton Church

At Thurgarton Church the sun
burns the winter clouds over
the gaunt Danish stone
and thatched reeds that cover
the barest chapel I know.

I could compare it with
the Norse longboats that bore
burning the body forth
in honour from the shore
of great fjords long ago.

The sky is red and cold
overhead, and three small
sturdy trees keep a hold
on the world and the stone wall
that encloses the dead below.

I enter and find I stand
in a great barn, bleak and bare;
like ice the winter ghosts and
the white walls gleam and flare
and flame as the sun drops low.

And I see, then, that slowly
the December day is gone.
I stand in the silence, not wholly
believing I am alone.
Somehow I cannot go.

Then a small wind rose, and the trees
began to crackle and stir
and I saw the moon by degrees
ascend in the window till her
light cut a wing in the shadow.

I thought: the House of the Dead.
The dead moon inherits it.
And I seem in a sense to have died
as I rise from where I sit
and out into darkness go.

I know as I leave I shall pass
where Thurgarton's dead lie
at those old stones in the grass
under the cold moon's eye.
I see the old bones glow.

No, they do not sleep here
in the long holy night of
the serene soul, but keep here
a dark tenancy and the right of
rising up to go.

Here the owl and the soul shriek with
the voice of the dead as they turn
on the polar spit and burn
without hope and seek with
out hope the holy home below.

Yet to them the mole and
mouse bring a wreath and a breath
of the flowering leaves of the soul,
and it is from the Tree of Death
these leaves of life grow.

The rain, the sometimes summer
rain in a memory of roses
will fall lightly and come a-
mong them as it erases
summers so long ago.

And the voices of those
once so loved will flitter
over the nettled rows
of graves and the holly trees twitter
like friends they used to know.

And not far away the
icy and paralysed stream
has found it also, that day the
flesh became glass and a dream
with nowhere to go.

Haunting the December
fields their bitter lives
entreat us to remember
the lost spirit that grieves
over these fields like a scarecrow.

That grieves over all it ever
did, and all, all not
done, that grieves over
its crosspurposed lot:
to know and not to know.

The masterless dog sits
outside the church door
with dereliction haunting its
heart that hankers for
the hand that it loved so.

Not in a small grave
outside the stone wall
will the love that it gave
ever be returned, not for all
time or tracks in the snow.

More mourned the death of the dog
than our bones ever shall
receive from the hand of god
this bone again, or all
that high hand could bestow.

As I stand by the porch
I believe that no one has heard
here in Thurgarton Church
one single veritable word
save the unspoken No.

The godfathered negative
that responds to our mistaken
incredulous and heartbroken
desire above all to live
as though things were not so.

Desire to live as though the
two footed clay stood up
proud never to know the
tempests that rage in the cup
under a rainbow.

Desire above all to live
as though the soul was stone
believing we cannot give
or love since we are alone
and always will be so.

That heartbroken desire
to live as though no light
ever set the seas on fire
and no sun burned at night
or Mercy walked to and fro.

The proud flesh howls: I am not
caught up in the great cloud
of my unknowing. But that
proud flesh has endowed
us with the cloud we know.

To this the unspoken No
of the dead god responds
and then the whirlwinds blow
over all things and beyond
and the dead mop and mow.

And there in the livid dust
and bones of death we search
until we find as we must
outside Thurgarton Church
only wild grasses blow.

I hear the old bone in me cry
and the dying spirit call:
I have forfeited all
and once and for all must die
and this is all that I know.

For now in a wild way we
know that Justice is served
and that we die in the clay we
dread, desired and deserved,
awaiting no judgement day.

George Barker

Aldborough Mill

Margaret Tidy (née Cooke) "He sold the building to the Pataks for the great sum of £5000. It was a disaster, getting rid of it."

We tried to assemble as full a list as we could of people who had been employed at the mill within the memory of those to whom we spoke.

People employed at the mill
Charles Tidy
George Hobbs
Leslie Green
Florence Glister
Albert Amis
Ken Douglas
Janet Duffield
Milly Chapman
Dorothy Strange
Lillian Hicks
Kathleen Spinks
Alfred Green
Audrey Eagling
Lewis Eagling
Sarah Glister
Romany Temple
Fred Hall
Joan Starling
Enid Grey
Winifred Underwood
Ernest Lambert
Mr & Mrs Williamson
Mr & Mrs McCoombe
Mr & Mrs Carr
Herbert Harmer
Almer Barber
Jack Money
Len Eke
Arthur Gray
John Hall
Sidney Woodcock
Sidney Jickells
Mr Baronic

In 1964 Thomas Cooke sold Aldborough Mill to Patak Spices Ltd, a company which mixed spices and made pickles. At first sight, this seems somewhat strange. For over forty years he had run a successful business, in economic circumstances which were rarely favourable. However, he did benefit from a stable and captive workforce, to whom he paid low wages (in their estimate!) and to whom he refused access to unions. In spite of this, however, he was regarded as a man who was always fair in his dealings. When he came to sell to Patak, Thomas Cooke himself had been experimenting in aromatics, as his family recalled. It was clear that traditional milling could no longer sustain a business nor provide a livelihood for his employees; but at the same time, a company already established in a field to which he felt drawn might yet maintain the mill as a place of continued production and employment. And in his middle sixties, perhaps he felt rather tired. For a few years, the mill did indeed prosper again, as in fact Patak prospered. They bought the buildings at a very attractive price, and inherited a loyal workforce, inured to low wages. In hindsight, that seems a shrewd move.

Patak are now established at national level as market leaders in their range of products.

With the closing of Aldborough Mill a significant element of Aldborough life came to an end.

In 1981 Aldborough Mill was converted into three houses.

The Last Quarter
1975 - 2000

The Community Centre	140
Bill Howett	141
Reg Hunn	141
Sport	142
Tug-of-War	142
Cricket	143
Knight's	143
Football	144
Aldborough Village Show	145
Billy Hammond	145
Around the Green	146
The Parish Council	149
Tinkers Close	150
Places of Worship	150
Prince Andrew's Chapel	150
Aldborough Church	150
Extension to the churchyard	151
Thurgarton Church	151
The Methodist Chapel	152
The Surgery	152
A Brief Tour of the Community	153
Environment, Footpaths, Conservation Areas	154
Business, The Shops	154
The Pubs, Youth, Elders, Community Life	155
Twinning	156
The School	157

Community Centre

David Cooke fills in the background to the campaign to convert the old Temperance Hall into the Community Centre.

David Cooke "Back in the late 1960s, I was Youth Club leader for the area; well, we were very short of facilities to run the club - which had quite good membership at that time - so we just thought to ourselves that Aldborough Mill, still under my Uncle Tom, was just not using the old Temperance Hall and Coffee Room Company Ltd. The plain fact is it was redundant; Barclays Bank, who used part of the house weekly as a bank, had pulled out some years earlier; my aunt, who had lived in the house, had moved out by this time; the main hall itself, which even had seed dressers and things like that in it, was becoming rat-infested and so on. I just wondered whether we could use part of this as a youth club. I approached my uncle, Tom Cooke, who thought it might be a possibility."

Discussions got under way involving Tom and Oliver Cooke, and attempts were made to contact representatives of the original families who had founded the Temperance Hall. The legal aspect to this was handled by Cedric Brown, a solicitor in Aylsham. The formal offer of the building to the parish was made in 1970.

David Cooke "By this time, the whole thing had moved far beyond the idea of just a Youth Club. The Dept of Environment and the Dept of Education and Science, said that if we could raise a 25% deposit, then the remaining 75% would come from public funds. They insisted that it should be developed on their lines, as a full community centre, with facilities for youth work included. So we had various public meetings at that time, and with the help of Cedric Brown we set things up accordingly."

A Public Meeting was held to discuss the idea, and unanimous support was forthcoming. A Community Centre Management Committee was founded, and money-raising events of all kinds were held, dances in the Church Room, fêtes on the Green, sewing groups.

Kath Howett "I've got a picture of Bill bowling for a pig, we also had somebody who had a miniature train."

Architects and builders were engaged, conversion work undertaken, the day came for the opening, November 26, 1976. It was clearly something of a 'flagship' operation at the time, as the line-up of dignitaries on the stage indicates.

Sir Edmund Bacon, Lord Lieutenant of Norfolk, Mr J.P. Winter, chairman of Norfolk County Council, Mr M, Chaplin, chairman of Norfolk Education Committee. In his speech, Sir Edmund said, "These days, 'village' is rather a dirty word. People say they are not economically viable, but a village is the life of the countryside."

*Management Committee
Nov 1976*

*Geoffrey Fisher (Chairman)
David Cooke (Vice Chairman)
Reg Hunn (Treasurer & Gen. Mgr)
Bill Howett (Bar Administrator)
and members:
Charles Matts
Mr H. Holman
Dr C. Skipper
Dick Price
Richard Riley
Mrs Chamberlain
Mrs J. Price
Mrs J. Halliday
Mrs W. Spurrell
Mrs D. Reynolds*

And the village had a hard time raising £8750, their share of the total cost of £35,000. Even with all the money-raising efforts of the previous five years, they were still £3000 short at the time of opening; but brave individuals were prepared to be generous.

David Cooke "Members of the committee had to stand Sam for borrowing money from the banks."

For Kath Howett the strong memory of those days is backed up by evidence.

Kath Howett "I've still got a letter at home that Bill had to sign as trustee - that's why they worked so hard to make sure the thing worked!"

And work they did, in many, many ways to ensure the money was paid off! Jean Price was greatly involved at this time.

Jean Price "The tug-of-war boys used to have magnificent feasts there - everybody used to fight to get tickets for those; they had a dozen or more courses, and the boys all used to serve, we had a fantastic evening. This was in the early years after it opened. The first one they actually had in the Church Room; people used to come from all over to get these tickets."

One club which was particularly strong in the early days of the Centre was the Old Time and Sequence Dancing Club.

Kath Howett "It was started by Jack and Betty Money, of Thurgarton Street - they were both very 'charismatic' as leaders. We'd meet on Thursday night throughout year, except for a four-week break in summer. Very often we combined with clubs from Holt, North Walsham and Overstrand. And then every so often there would be a 'long' night, when men wore evening dress and the ladies wore long dresses. Sadly, Jack died from a heart attack in 1984..."

Bill Howett

Notes Bill and Kath Howett came to the village in 1956, and although strictly in terms of parish boundaries they live in Alby, they always felt Aldborough was closer. Bill played in the cricket team for a number of years, and from the outset was very committed to the Community Centre campaign and determined that the venture should be a success. He was the ideal Bar Manager - he didn't drink!

Reg Hunn

Notes Reg was born in the village, and lived all his adult life in Aldborough, apart from the war years. (He was POW in Italy and Austria.) As we have seen, he played football and cricket for village sides, but sport was not his only area of involvement. He was a Parish Councillor, and in the early sixties he ran the Youth Club, which was the place for Aldborough girls to meet Gresham boys - five marriages resulted from those evenings with frothy coffee and jiving! In his later years he was manager of the Community Centre.

Sport
Tug-of-War

The Black Boys' Tug-of-War team thrived for over ten years, under the leadership of Dick Price, who'd learnt about the sport in his National Service days. Their first contest sobered them up.

Dick Price "Alby Horseshoes had quite a decent side, they were beating all and sundry round this way, they challenged us and they pulled us all over the park! We weren't too pleased about that, so we decided to put in some training."

You didn't make the team if you were puny of mind or muscle.

Dick Price "We put up a training rig on what is now the car park behind the Community Centre; that was three telegraph poles like a big tripod, quite high, then we had a forty-gallon drum filled with concrete; we cut it into three, had a big rod through the middle, so you could put one, two or three sections on; then we put some hundredweights on top of it as well, when we were getting a bit more proficient. Then, after two or three goes, we were able to beat the Three Horseshoes!"

There was no stopping them! They started beating the big Norfolk teams like Reedham and Cawston, and winning all the local fêtes; next step was to join the Amateur Athletics Association and compete in contests further afield. These outings became family events, everybody travelling by coach. Dick's wife Jean recalls these trips.

Jean Price "At one time, you see, the tug-of-war was such a family-orientated sport, believe it or not, the families always used to go with them at weekends; we'd go all over the place by bus, mothers and the children."

On one occasion they were invited to pull in Holland.

Dick Price "We did all right for a start, we were doing quite well; the English style of pulling, you get very low, that's a kind of pressure-pulling; that worked for us for a start, we watched these Dutch teams, and they were all big heaves, big pulls, you know, we could hold that, we was all right, but what we didn't know was what the ground was like; while there was turf on, we were OK, but after a while, of course, the turf go, and that was pure sand underneath - you couldn't hold your feet, you just slipped through it all the time; in the end we were nearly knee-deep!"

And the Black Boys tug-of-war team make a foot-note in the history of Norfolk marathon-running.

Jean Price "They were always doing things, weren't they? Something else, too, as regards to the tug-of-war team - they really

Aldborough Tug-of-War team.

Mervyn Burton-Pye
Bob Beale
David Rowe
Reggie Amis
John Howard
Rodney Thompson
Alan Wright
Leslie Amis
Dick Price

were the ones who started off this marathon from Kelling to Norwich; they did a fun run to raise money for Kelling, with the nurses riding on bikes against the boys who ran; then we all gathered at the Black Boys afterwards and had a jolly good time. The fellow Shrive thought what a good idea it was, and he started off the other one."

John Shrive started the Norfolk marathon

*Aldborough First Team Mansell Stevenson Div II winners 2000
Back row: Andy Nash, Kevin Bacon, Jimmy Lewis, Damien Fahy, Neil Briggs, Jimmy Nichol
Front row: Willy Frazer, Ashley Barnard, Tony Fell (Capt.), Ben Sizeland, Eddie Downing*

Cricket

The Black Boys again became the home of the cricket team. Earlier, as we have seen, it was based in the Red Lion, and then the Community Centre for a while. Here are some interesting facts and figures about particular teams and players who have featured over the years.

Most successful season - 1986. Won Lady Mary Trophy and Michael Wright Cup.

Most prestigious match - Competing in the Carter Cup in 1987/88, having won the Lady Mary trophy the previous season. Played against North Runcton and Swardeston - both teams being in Norfolk's top division.

Highest score - Geoff Chamberlain, 200 not out against Gothic. Aldborough still lost the game!

Best bowling figures - Ron Dobbie 8 for 30, mid-sixties.

Biggest hit - Sandy Kenyon, Norwich City goal-keeper, mid-seventies. Cleared Days' shop, landing in the back garden.

Most notable player - Clive Radley (Norfolk, Middlesex and England), as a very young man.

Worst season - (year unknown) bottom of 2nd Division of Alliance, then relegated to Norfolk League.

Most exciting finish - in 2000, a touring side, St Margaretsbury from Hertfordshire scored 254. The Aldborough side also scored 254, with Chris Lewis being run out on the last ball!

Longest-serving captain - Reggie Hunn, 1946-60.

Best cricket teas - By overwhelming vote, Jean Halliday in the Community Centre!

Knight's Sporting Memorabilia Auctions

A love of cricket has led to a thriving new business for one Aldborough resident. As chairman of the cricket club in 1993 Tim Knight held an auction of cricket-related memorabilia to boost club funds. The auction of around 200 donated lots attracted an unexpected amount of interest from out of the village and raised over £3000. Knight's is now a key auction house in sporting memorabilia and has sold many thousands of items including the bat used by Ian Botham to score 149 not out against the Australians in 1981 at Headingley and the gloves worn by Brian Lara when he scored his world record score of 501.

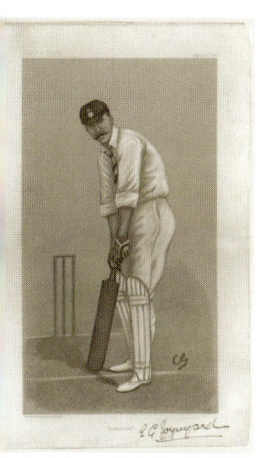

Vanity Fair cricket print

Here is a tribute from Chris Lewis, Chairman of Aldborough Cricket Club, to two of the club's mainstays in the second half of the century.

Chris Lewis For a cricket club as old as Aldborough to survive both financially and physically, it needs devoted custodians. There have been many people in the life of the club who have contributed a tremendous amount, but none more so than Reggie Hunn and Ron Dobbie. Both living in Aldborough, they managed the club from before the war to the present day. Reggie was the longest-serving skipper of all time, operating before and after the Second World War, when I suspect the club might have disappeared. Ron has worked tirelessly as Secretary/Treasurer and groundsman of great skill. The club trophies record their legendary playing achievements during this period. We should like to both acknowledge and thank them.

Ron Dobbie

Photo courtesy of EDP

Football

Bertie Cook has been associated with football in the village since he played for the junior team while a pupil at the village school. Following war service he lived in Goose Lane, Alby, before moving to Harmer's Lane, Thurgarton in 1953, where he has lived ever since. He played for Aldborough between 1947 and 1970, finally hanging up his boots at the age of 49. Following his retirement from the pitch he took up life on the touch-line as coach. For much of this time the team was run and sponsored by Billy Brett of the Black Boys. Bob Bishop took over as secretary in 1960, a position he held until 1995. He also ran the line with his famous bucket and sponge! In later years, sponsorship was taken over by the Red Lion. Here is a team photo from 1988. Best seasons were: 1979-81, North-East Norfolk League, second division, runners-up to the League Cup four times between 1980-91, runners-up to the League 81-82 /90-91 won Second Division League Cup in 1985-86

Aldborough Football Club 1988
Back row:
Patti Custerman (sponsor), Graham Gladden, Steve Haynes, Alan Witham, Tommy Glister, Stephen Hagan, Steve Cooke, Bob Bishop (sec.)
Front row:
Kevin Mason, Ian Brown, Mark Durrant, Will Howett, Paul Cox, Richard West, Mark Lambert

The original Committee
Steve Cushing
Ken Webb (Black Boys)
Barry Fowler
David Waine
Ron Hayton
Ron Henshaw
Richard Leeds
Angie Palmer
Chris Turner

Aldborough Village Show

The first Trade and Leisure Fair was held in 1983, in a bid both to raise money for charity and at the same time raise the profile of the community. The idea from the outset was to donate half of any profit made to a nominated charity in North Norfolk, with the other half available for Aldborough and Thurgarton. As it happened, the first year just managed to avoid a deficit. However, invaluable lessons had been learned, and in the following years the show increased in size and range, and showed a profit year on year; by the end of the century, over £90,000 had been raised.

In 1996, the name of the event was changed to the Aldborough Village Show. Since 1984 it has funded the Christmas tree which stands on the Green. In the photo Father Christmas is enjoying a ride in Richard King's Buttercup on his way to meet the large crowd of children - over 100 - awaiting his arrival. He gives each child a small present, paid for out of Aldborough Village Show funds. Over the years many different individuals have made a huge contribution to the success of the Show, and have been involved in money-raising events round the year.

Billy Hammond

Notes A common sight when Norfolk is in holiday mood is Billy Hammond driving one of his prized vintage farm machines or traction engines. Billy is proud of the family connection with the Burrell traction engine works at Thetford (indeed, his father's Christian name was Burrell). He has been gradually adding to his collection making restoration his major priority. He is happy both to show his collection to visiting groups and to allow it to be featured in money-raising events for charity. Among his most prized possessions are three early tractors made in 1935, and a 1912 Burrell traction engine made in Thetford.

Around the Green

Greenacre built c1960
Welcome Cottage built 1988

Bone & Co bought by Albert Tash, Wilfred and Leslie Kent. Arthur Tash died 1970; Kent brothers then closed the shop in 1971. The premises were sold to Arthur Wright; they were left empty for 5 years, and then were restored by Marion and Alan Wright.
Thatched Gallery let to Charles Matts (furniture) 1986-87, Mother Goose (clothes) 1990-92, Julie Pryor (upholstery), Knights Sporting Auctions 1995-present day
Ivy Cottage
Two
Toby's Cottage

Manor Cottage
Butcher's Spurgeon sold to Leonard Massingham; his sons Clifford and Richard ran the shop until they sold it to Mr and Mrs Lanham January, 1984.
Rose Cottage

Old Bakery Cottage Broadgate Printers bought the old bakery c1980, left Aldborough in 1989. Steve Cushing (heating engineer) 1990-present day
St Anne's Cottage

John Brown's House
Chesterfield House When Ruth Bayes came to live here in 1981, she discovered that the first name on the deeds, very nearly 300 years ago, was Phoebe Bayes!

Sunholme
Mr Reynolds ran the honey cart until sewers were installed in the mid 1950s
Greenview
Eastview

Black Boys
May, 1949 Arthur Godley
May, 1955 Arthur Garnett Brett
1969 It became a Steward and Patteson pub. Later, it was owned by Watney Mann, then Brent Walker.
It became a free house in 2000.

Spring House Geoffrey Fisher retired from the shop in 1987. It was bought by Brian and Sue Metcalf - house, shop, general store, fish and chips, garage, filling-station.
1990 - the general shop closed, continued trading as DIY shop.
1992 - DIY shop, petrol pumps closed.
1992 - converted to residential use

Note When Brian Metcalf removed the boarding that had covered the two side windows, he found Jimmy Colman's hooks in the window frames. There were 500 in total. Top rows for repaired watches/bottom rows for watches awaiting repair.

Fernleigh House
The Old Post Office
Chapman's Row 1, 2 & 3

Wright's Cottage Original demolished and a new house built on the site in the mid 90s.
2nd Slip
1st Slip
Long Stop

The Stables Sally Ann Hair Fashions (opened by the Wright family) Closed 1986.
Days' Shop

The brothers Day bow out, 1979.
1979 shop sold to Jim and Doreen Wright
1982 shop sold to Ron and Elaine Hayton
2000 shop sold to Tony and Margot Roper
2000 shop sold to Lynn and Rodney Hurn

Perrotts (previously South View) built by Bob Williamson, farmer at Manor Farm Thurgarton, brother to Jack Williamson, tailor. The window was designed for watching cricket. Dr Eddy moved here in 1981.
Old Post Office Stores
Run by Elsie and Derrick Davison between 1955 and 1983
Cobblers Rest built 1990 by Elsie and Derrick Davison
Post Office moved here late 1987. It is now run by Peter Davison and sister Brenda.

Butterfly Cottage built early 90s. Bed and Breakfast as from 1997 run by Janet Davison.
Stonecroft
The Bungalow
Barley Cottage
Community Centre

Victoria Cottage
Fox Cottage
Greenside

Nelson House built in the late 80s.
Wenspur
Whistlestop
The Tannery
Virginia Cottage
Kent's Place Baldwin's shop closed 1969; block bought by Leslie Kent.

Village Antiques Kents' General Store sold to Gerald Round 1972. David and Margaret Waine bought the business in 1980, continued trading until 1983. Terry Holdgate opened Village Antiques in 1984
Apple Cottage
Cricketers' Rest

The Old Bakehouse
Old Red Lion - changed into restaurant in the late 60s. In the mid 80s Marcelle Eyles and daughter Patti took over the business. Patti's Italian husband Bruno was chef. Permission sought to add licence as public house in the mid-90s.

St Joseph's Mead built late 60s.
The Firs built early 1974

The Church Room Kitchen refitted 2000.
Lark Rise built late 60s

Tudor Rose built late 60s
Lumley built late 60s

Haven built 70s. Oliver Cooke lived here in his later years.
Gargoyles built mid 90s

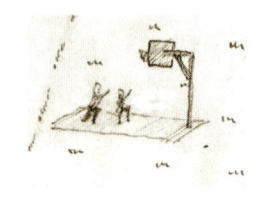

The Basketball court was provided in January 2000.

And just off the Green...

Cookes David Cooke's Tractors closed in the village in 1995 and moved to a new site on the A140 at Alby. The building was demolished, together with the old fire station, which had been converted into a house called Pipits. Eventually the land was used for a development of eight houses, Pipits' Close.

The Parish Council

A major anomaly in the administrative affairs of Aldborough was resolved in the 1990. Discussions had been taking place for years between the Parish Council and the lawyers of the Hon. Doris Harbord, the Lady of Hanworth manor. The issue was simple: who owns the Green? It was reported in the EDP as far back as June 1973.

The lord of a Norfolk manor opposed the claim by a lady of the neighbouring manor to the ownership of a North Norfolk beauty spot yesterday. The ownership of Aldborough Green was disputed at a sitting in Norwich of a Commons Commissioner, Mr A. A. Baden Fuller. Ownership was claimed both by the Hon. Doris Harbord, of Gunton Park, Hanworth, the Lady of Hanworth manor and the trustees of the Gunton estate, and Aldborough Parish Council. Appearing for the Parish Council were Mr G.D. Fisher, of the Green, Aldborough, and Mr E. C. Lilly, a former member of this council and a member of Erpingham Rural District Council, of Corner House, Wickmere, the lord of the manor of Aldborough. Mr. N. Craig for Miss Harbord and the trustees, said there was no complete reference to Aldborough Green or a complete breakdown of the Gunton Estate in the deeds. 'Over the years there has been a travelling fair which pays a rental for the village green. This gets submitted back to our client, and has been for many years,' he said. He submitted statements from a former clerk to the Parish Council and agent to the estate, saying the fair tolls were divided between the estate and the Parish Council. Mr Charles Pull, representing Irelands, the present agents, said a proportion of the tolls had continued to be paid to the estate. Mr Fisher said he understood Miss Harbord had manorial rights, but had never heard she was the owner. 'I understand the tolls were collected on behalf of the Parish Council,' he said. Mr Lilly said the estate had never made any direct contribution or any renovation to the Green, and no member of the estate was on the committee set up after the war to restore the Green. 'I am lord of the manor of Aldborough and received certain dues, but that did not mean I claimed ownership of the land. She has rights over the Green but has not got ownership. Ownership, I always thought, was vested in the owners of the property around the Green,' he said. The commissioner said, 'If she is the owner of the manor I think she must be owner of the Green.. The basic fact is this lady of the manor has been receiving money for the Green.' He will give his decision in writing at a later date.

Ownership of the Green was eventually transferred to the Parish Council in 1990.

Here is the Hon. Doris Harbord seated on the bench placed on the Green to mark the Queen's Jubilee in 1977.

Billy Hammond and Geoffrey Fisher at the official opening of Tinkers Close

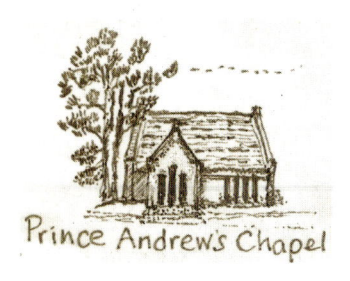

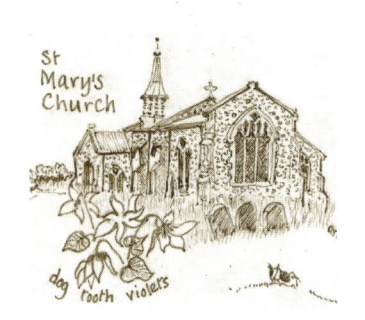

Tinkers Close

On June 10, 1988 the North Norfolk News reported the start to a major housing scheme for Aldborough; thirteen houses and four bungalows were built; Tinkers Close came into being.

Tinkers Close Residents Association was formed to improve the area in front of the houses, to make it a safe and attractive place for the children to play. They raised money themselves by a sponsored parachute-jump; they received a grant of £250 from the North Norfolk District Council in October, 1999 and a similar sum from Aldborough Millennium Committee, which they used to buy good quality play equipment, fencing and raised garden beds.

Places of Worship

Prince Andrew's Chapel

I do believe John Brown has featured in every section of this book! David Cooke here tells one of the stipulations of his last will and testament.

David Cooke "John Brown was a unique old man; he was a JP, a registrar and so on, but my father and uncle who were leaders in the Brethren, always wanted him to sell them the land (which went with his house) where the Gospel Hall stood. But he would not do that, no way, he would collect his little bit of rent. As the years went on, there seemed to be a certain amount of acrimony about all this, and John Brown would not shift; but when he died, he left provision in his will - and very clear instructions with his daughter - that Oliver Cooke was to be approached about this, that Oliver Cooke was to be given the first option on his house and all the land that went all up the back. And so my father bought it. The trustees of the Gospel Hall were then able to purchase from my father sufficient land on which Prince Andrew's Chapel now stands."

A long period of fund-raising resulted in the building of the new chapel. It was designed by Richard Mendes-Houlston and built by Jacobs & Gee.

Aldborough Church

Notes When the Revd Frank Irwin left in 1980, he had been not just the Rector of Aldborough with Thurgarton, but also of Bessingham and of Hanworth with Gunton. Both Thurgarton and Gunton had recently been put in the care of the Redundant Churches Fund. A new Rectory had been on the agenda for some years; in 1977 the Diocesan authorities had approved a plan to build on land already owned next to Aldborough churchyard, but the North Norfolk District Council refused planning permission. There was a very long period without a Rector. One retired priest, the Revd Eric Moreton, was already living in Alby; another, Canon Charles Bayes, came to live in Aldborough in 1981, and together with the help of Reg Clark, a lay Reader, they kept services going during this interregnum. The lack of suitable housing was a problem in attracting a new incumbent. Then, without local consultation, the Diocesan

The last wedding to take place at St Mary's Church in the year 2000 was that of James Wright and Tracy Jones

authorities exchanged Thurgarton Rectory for a house in Hanworth, which prospective candidates found unsuitable for use as a rectory on account of its size, location and internal planning. In 1982 the living was still vacant. Another factor was that none of the parishes in the group had succeeded in paying their quota in full (this is now known as Parish share). When Bessingham and Hanworth agreed to join the Roughton group, Aldborough could not survive financially as a separate parish. The only solution was to join the Erpingham group which had recently acquired the parishes of Thwaite and Alby (with Alby church closed). In 1983 the Revd David Pope, Rector of Erpingham and Calthorpe, became priest in charge of Aldborough with Thurgarton; in April 1985 he retired, having been heard to say that Aldborough was the last straw. The next interregnum was not quite so long. The Revd Barry Middleton came late in 1985 and soon had Ingworth added to the group. When he left in January 1992 there was another year without a parish priest until the arrival of the Revd Brian Faulkner in January 1993. Alby church was soon re-opened, so there are six active churches in this benefice, with the Rector living in Erpingham.

Extension to the churchyard

The churchyard had become full for burials, a situation which gave the PCC the option of either closing it or extending into land already owned by the church, given by the Lilly family for this purpose. In spite of the ever-increasing expense of maintenance, the PCC decided that this was an important service to the parish and the churchyard was extended in 1990.

Thurgarton Church

By 1976, a combination of factors brought a critical moment of decision to the small group of worshippers at All Saints'. There were only ten names on the Electoral Roll, and the roof was in urgent need of repair. The Rector, the Revd Frank Irwin said that 'he did not see that Thurgarton Church was necessary as a Parish Church'; so began the process of offering the church to the Redundant Churches Fund (now called the Churches Conservation Trust). In September 1976 large sums of money were left quite anonymously in the collecting boxes, but not enough to save the church, which closed in December of that year.

Subsequently, restoration work was undertaken and the church is now used for worship two or three times a year.

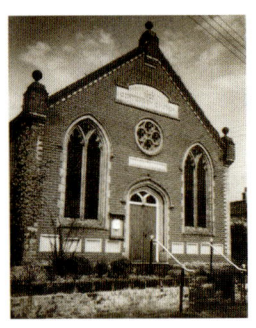

The Methodist Chapel

The Methodist Chapel

The Methodist chapel, whose initial building costs proved something of a burden to its congregation, continued its role as a place of worship for over ninety years. But in 1998, it was forced to close. At about this time, the Methodist minister, Don Moxon, wrote the following.

Revd Don Moxon The members of Aldborough Methodist Church recently came to the sad conclusion that they are no longer able to maintain themselves as a separate worshipping congregation; in consequence, services at the chapel have now ceased and permission is being sought from the relevant Methodist authorities to sell the building. There are two main reasons for this. Firstly, the infirmity of many of the members makes it either impossible or dangerous to negotiate the steep steps to the chapel, and secondly, the costs of repairing or maintaining the building have become prohibitive for the small congregation. Attempts to maintain separate Methodist worship by holding services in the Church Room or in Prince Andrew's Chapel have not really succeeded.

The Surgery

Dr Philip Wood came to Aldborough in 1988 and worked as Dr Skipper's assistant until 1992, when he took over the practice. During his time of training in Norwich he'd often driven up the A140 and wondered where the sign to Aldborough led - and now he found out! He also discovered the reality behind the phrase 'single-handed doctor'.

Dr Wood "Colin did everything; he sat at his desk, he saw the patients, he answered the phone, went into the dispensary and dispensed the drugs, it was quite remarkable; he had no attached staff at all."

Taking over the practice, however, meant finding suitable premises, and effectively that entailed building a new surgery. An unlikely location off the Thwaite Road proved a temporary solution.

The three doctors at Dr Skipper's retirement party in the Community Centre.

Dr Wood "We had the portakabins in the farmyard very kindly provided by Billy Hammond, who was enormously supportive and helpful - we were there about two years."

In 1990 the Government introduced a new contract to general medical practice; these entailed taking on more staff as well as computerising the administration. He started planning, too, for the new surgery, which came to open in 1994. In the meantime, his list-size had grown.

Dr Wood "I inherited about 1750 from Colin, and we're now between 2200 and 2300 - the national average is about 1800 - it's big."

Two factors have enabled him to cope with the workload.

Dr Wood "It's only sustainable because I've help, Peter Harvey coming in a day a week. We also have help from a lady doctor - in fact there have been three over the last two or three years, they all seem to emigrate to New Zealand!"

The other major difference is the new co-operative venture between local practices, introduced to ease the burden of out-of-hours work.

Dr Wood "All the local GPs got together to form the North-East Norfolk Doctors' Co-operative set up in 1995."

Other major changes in external factors have also had a positive effect. Local practices are now administered within a locally based Primary Care Trust.

Dr Wood "This has been a good thing; practices work together very well, we share ideas and resources, if we have a problem we can discuss it."

The Surgery

He now works with a team of between eight and ten attached staff, who form a contemporary rural practice which is a model of its kind.

Dr Wood "I think this is worth saying, Aldborough as a practice has a high reputation within the Primary Care Group - very gratifying for me and my staff."

A Brief Tour of the Community at the end of the Century

The purpose of a book of this kind is not only to provide a history of the past, but also to provide information about present times for future historians! The following section has been compiled with this in mind.

The EDP Norfolk Best Kept Village Competition

Aldborough has entered the Norfolk Competition regularly since its introduction in 1966 and was a winner in 1978, 1979, 1997 and 1999. The village has also been runner-up, and been a finalist on many other occasions, as well as winning special section awards for Churchyard Conservation, Best Kept Village Green and Most Improved Entrant.

In 1997 Aldborough (population 575) was Norfolk's nomination for the National Village of the Year Award in the 'Villages over 500 population category'. The competition 'seeks to reward village communities which demonstrate ability and effort to enhance aspects of village life'.

Ruth Bayes & David Waine at the Awards' Ceremony in 1999, the second time Aldborough was chosen to represent Norfolk.

Result of 1997 competition *Aldborough was not the national winner (Coniston, Cumbria), nor did it win any of the individual categories. However, the judges were so impressed by the strength of Aldborough's submission they created an extra prize, the **Judges' Special Recommendation** for being an 'impressive all-rounder'.*

The competition, which was in its first year of operation, established the following areas for consideration: environment, business, youth, elders, and community life. We shall follow these categories, as laid out in the booklet which presented Aldborough's submission in 1997, using the information given then.

Environment

The village green is a greatly valued open space - its use and care are a source of pride. It is a social asset, being a natural centre as well as a cricket pitch and play area. Property owners are encouraged to plant trees and to seek appropriate advice on their and care. Support is given by the North Norfolk District Council. The Parish Council cares for the trees around the Green; oak trees awarded as a prize in a previous Best Kept Village competition are thriving. A large field on the outskirts of the village has been reclaimed and re-hedged and wild flowers are reappearing; children walking to school use the footpath which runs across this field.

Footpaths

Billy Hammond has been instrumental in ensuring that footpaths are open, fit to use and properly sign-posted. For several years he organised village walks to show local people where the footpaths were. Recently, Weavers Way was re-routed to pass through the village.

Special Conservation Areas

The churchyard is managed on conservation principles, and for three consecutive years won the Norfolk Wildlife Trust Churchyard Conservation Award. The older part is rich in spring bulbs, planted by a former rector a hundred years ago. A large area of dog's tooth violets is particularly treasured, as are fritillaries and common orchids. When the graveyard was extended in 1990 careful thought was given to tree-planting, hedging and seeding. The centre of the village and the area around the church are conservation areas. Planning applications are considered with this in mind.

Business

Conservation constraints mean that the Parish Council is not in a position to encourage new businesses, but it looks favourably on planning applications such as the use of barns for workshops combined with housing. The council makes a point of employing local people whenever possible.

The Shops

A.G. Davison, the Post Office has been run by members of the same family for fifty years. It offers in addition to expected postal services shoes, shoe repairs, clothing, haberdashery, dry-cleaning, toys, theatre tickets and Christmas trees.

Days' Stores, the Spar sell a wide range of quality foods; also video hire and video camera hire; weekly delivery area is over 100 sq miles.

K. & L. Lanham's, the Butcher offers top quality meat, plus a variety of cooked meats, eggs and ice cream. A delivery service is available.

Village Antiques Unusual presents are available and advice is freely given on all collectables.

The Pubs

The Black Boys and **The Old Red Lion** Both pubs have restaurants, serving a wide clientele.

Youth

A children's playground is provided at one end of the green and is maintained by the Parish Council, helped by local fund-raising. The Cricket Club runs a weekly session for youngsters and has established a junior team. They play 'kwik cricket' as well as the more conventional form. Tae Kwondo classes meet weekly and demonstrate their art annually at the Village Show.

The playgroup is still going strong after over twenty years. It started on March 1, 1977 in the top room of the Community Centre. Now it continues to give an excellent service under the name of Stepping Stones, and is based at Aldborough School.

Playgroup in 1978 run by Sue Allen (left) & Linda Mears (right)

Elders

Village Care was started in 1989 by Gabi Kleissner. On three Tuesdays each month, Village Care provides a lunch club in the Community Centre, a hot three-course meal at a good price. On the remaining Tuesday there is a meal at Prince Andrew's Chapel, and a coffee morning once a week. Village Care organises the car scheme and pays drivers' expenses. Patients are taken to medical appointments. Volunteer drivers collect meals-on-wheels from the school kitchen and deliver them twice a week, organised by the WRVS. The Over 60s group meets regularly for games such as whist and scrabble, has coffee evenings and arranges several annual outings. Village Care is not just for the elderly; it organises the Tae Kwondo classes, runs First Aid courses.

Gabi Kleissner

Much of the information on these two pages was taken from Aldborough's submission for the 1997 competition.

Community Life

The village newsletter, 'Keeping in Touch' is produced monthly to cover events in the six villages of the ecclesiastical grouping of parishes. It has been published since 1987 and is delivered free to every house, with expenses covered by donations and low-cost adverts from strictly local businesses.

The Community Bus service started in July, 1978 carrying out scheduled runs to Holt, Aylsham, Sheringham and North Walsham. By 1981, the service was carrying 6000 passengers per year. As ever, it relies on a team of volunteer drivers, all of whom have to take a PSV test before climbing up to take the wheel.

The Aldborough Players The first in a long string of annual performances by the Aldborough Players was **Sally in Pantoland** and residents look forward to this sparkle of theatrical sunshine in the depths of winter. Impresario Malcolm Ward was the driving force behind a string of successful productions and built a strong company that enabled later directors, producers and writers to entertain audiences with traditional storylines enhanced by strong local content.

Signposts in Villiers Saint Denis

140 different Aldborough people have visited Villiers (pop 600)
98 different Villiers people have come here (pop 800)

The first group visit to Villiers was made by the following people:- The Hammonds, the Batches, the Scargills, Jane Maguire and Ruth Bayes

Twinning

The last major initiative of the twentieth century was the drive to find a partner community on the continent. Signposts at each end of the village now announce the outcome of that campaign. The whole process started with a letter to the Parish Council from Ruth Bayes, in May, 1989, suggesting twinning with 'somewhere in Europe'.

Ruth Bayes "I felt there would be cultural benefit from the opportunity to get to know people from overseas. Early progress was very slow; our initial idea was to try for a twinning arrangement with a Dutch village, as historically there have always been close ties between East Anglia and the Netherlands. However, that came to nothing. But I was not the only one pressing us to link with a European community. Both Jane Maguire and Adrian Scargill were strong supporters from the outset, sure that the arrangement would be 'very good for the children'."

Twinning arrangements are set up through a body called the Local Government International Bureau, which acts as a 'marriage broker' for any community within Europe expressing a wish to be involved in this way. Aldborough's main criterion was that any 'twin' should be within a day's journey. Ruth continues:

Ruth Bayes "The French village of Villiers St Denis was suggested to us; Villiers lies on the river Marne between Paris and Reims, in the Champagne district. Jane Maguire offered to make an incognito visit late in 1989, and following this she reported back positively to the Aldborough steering group. The first group visit as such was from Villiers, and took place in July 1991. We made our first visit in October, 1991; there were, admittedly, some early misunderstandings and reservations - partly to do with different civic systems in the two countries. These were largely resolved, although not all Aldborough residents wanted to go ahead with the scheme."

It was decided to proceed, but without asking for any money from Parish funds. The only public money available was a small grant from the EU to help with transport costs. The official ceremonies at our end took place in October, 1995, with a concert of music and dance in the school hall organised by Gwynneth Bailey and performed by some of the children. The following morning, a Communion Service was held in St Mary's, followed by speeches, Twinning Oaths and national anthems in the Community Centre. Then everybody moved on to the barn at Manor Farm, where they were hosted by Billy Hammond. Adrian Scargill wrote this about the occasion.

Adrian Scargill We arrived in the barn to the smell of jacket potatoes and the sound of the No Name Band. The barn looked wonderful and was a tribute to the efforts of the Twinning Committee and helpers. Over the next three hours an excellent meal was served and eaten, and the wine and champagne (a gift from the French) flowed. By late afternoon, the number in the barn was approaching 200... and there was a wonderful atmosphere. The evening concluded with a firework display in the adjacent field.

Billy Hammond and the Mayor of Villiers shake hands on the bench that Aldborough presented to Villiers as a gift.

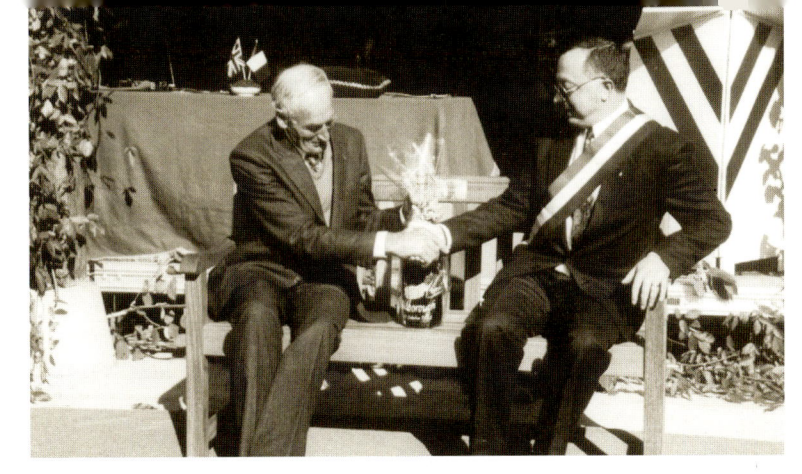

As a permanent seal on the twinning arrangement between the two communities, gifts were exchanged. On our visit to the official ceremonies in Villiers, we presented them with a bench, which has been installed in their main street. They in turn presented us with an antique wine press placed on the Green in front of the Church Room.

The School

In the last ten years of the century the government imposed the National Curriculum on children and their teachers. This restricted the opportunities for originality and creativity in teaching. Despite this, Aldborough Primary School has consistently performed well in National League tables while resolutely maintaining the ethos that the development of the individual is of greater importance than any statistic. The stability and commitment of the teaching and support staff during this period is to be applauded and we thank them for giving our children such an excellent start in life.

As a final entry we asked Adrian Scargill, head of Aldborough Primary School since 1989, to reflect on the nature of his role as we move into the new century.

Adrian Scargill In these early years of the twenty-first century, the role of the headteacher is probably more complex than it has ever been. We live in a world that is changing at an ever-increasing pace, and it is vital that schools are able to make sense of what is happening. At the same time, we need to provide some stability for children who may increasingly come from troubled homes and backgrounds. The demands on children, teachers and everybody working in education have never been greater, and consequently the head teacher has a key role in shaping what happens in our schools. Paramount is the need to foster a set of values and attitudes which children will take into adult life, where there is tolerance of other races, cultures and religions. We need to educate our children to care about their immediate environment and to lead them to take a positive role in both their own and the earth's future.

Aldborough Primary School - Whole School Photograph 1995

Starting top left and moving to right then back to left roughly following each row.

Staff and Governors
Terry Thacker (deputy headteacher)
Adrian Scargill (headteacher)
Rosie Procter (Dickens) Claire Taylor
Sue Mumford Dr P. Wood Phyllis Davison
Julie Bobbin Maureen Bane
Deborah Williams Carolyn Tingay
Penny Jackson Pam Pickthall Sue Jones
Carrie Lawson Marion Cox
Gaye Westacott Jill Morgan Roger Legge
(Chairman of Governors) Karen Fidgen
Heather Attew Maureen Rogers
Gwynneth Bailey is absent

Pupils
Daniel Thomas Matthew Guise
Tom Brocklehurst Alexandra Mackenzie
Wesley Attew Ben Thomas Joanne Filby
Theo Leeds Adam Cook Paul Colman
Damien Woolard Ian Thirtell
Benjamin Radley Annie Ledsham-Darter
Sophy Clarke Daniel Witham Nick Taylor
Ben Kovacevic Emily Spray Owen Pugh
Mark Surridge William Peverill
Oliver Dean Darren Hall Chris Willis
Kylie Haynes Oliver Legge
Christian Attew Sam Bailey Jason Hall
Edward Taylor Laura Woolard
Sarah Hadlow Rachel Summons
Cheryl Turvey Chris Turner George Betts
Robert Tingay Leigh Colman
Amy Gulvin Lisa-Marie Cox Samantha Filby Johnathan Tipple Krystie-Anne Green Alan Morrison Glen Thirtell
James Attew Jody Radley Justin Turvey
Hayley Sadler Paula Carr Alice Mumford
Elaine Tamplin Celia Goodenough Robert Witham Terry Thomas Matthew Brocklehurst Alice Pugh Catherine Clarke
Pita Dixon Stephanie Watts Alex Ash
Donna Crispen Charlotte Willis Araminta Jackson Stephanie Burton-Pye unknown
Louise Wilmott Mathew Bundock
Rhiannon Lister Charles Betts
David Summons Jack Watts
Rachael Morrison Louise Morrison
Luke Welham Darren Turner
Catie Haynes Toby Hendry Luke Attew
Tom Cox Holly Towers Timmy Bunting
Natasha Wilmott Charlotte Middleton
Hannah King Ben Goodman
Ben Pierssone Jimmy-Lee Bundock
Joanne Haggith Megan Hennig
Hannah Esselmont Emrys Green
William Taylor Briony Welham
Chloe Gulvin Hannah Lawson
Beth Mumford Christopher Stacey
Michael Carr

Fernleigh Old Post Office Chapmans Row Wright's Cottage 2nd Slip 1st Slip Long Stop The Stables looking North

Black Boys Spring House

looking West

Sunholme Greenview Eastview

John Brown's House Chesterfield House

Old Bakery Cottage St Annes Cottage

Manor Cottage Lanhams Rose Cottage

The Thatched Gallery Ivy Cottage Two Tobys Cottage

Greenacre Welcome Cottage ALDBOROUGH Tudor Rose

Stone House • Perrotts • The Old Post Office Stores • Cobblers Rest • Post Office • Butterfly Cottage • Stonecroft • The Bungalow • Barley Cottage • Community Centre

The Forge

looking East

Victoria Cottage • Fox Cottage • Greenside

Nelson House • Wenspur • Whistlestop • The Tannery • Virginia Cottage • Kent's Place

Village Antiques • Cricketers Rest • Apple Cottage • undertakers • The Old Bakehouse • Red Lion

St. Josephs Mead • The Firs • Church Room • Larkrise

Aldborough Twinning Association
This antique wine press was given to the village by Villiers Saint Denis to mark the twinning of the two villages.

N W E S

The Haven • Gargoyle House

looking south

ALDBOROUGH

Acknowledgements

The Aldborough Village History Society wishes to thank the many people who helped their research for this book. We list below those who gave interviews, photographs, documents, postcards and memories. We apologise to anyone that we may have inadvertently omitted: everyone's contribution was vital.

Jane Amis	*Elsie Davison*	*Steve Haynes*	*Dick Price*
Cyril Bacon	*Peter Davison*	*Ron Hayton*	*Rose Purdy*
Harry Bane	*Audrey Day*	*Kath Howett*	*Janice Single*
Maureen Bane	*Anthony Day*	*Will Howett*	*Colin Skipper*
Tony Barber	*Joyce Day*	*Sue Hudson*	*Adrian Scargill*
Frank Benzie	*Ron Dobbie*	*Esmé Hurn*	*Gwen Smith*
Jean Benzie	*Queenie Douglas*	*Ida Impson*	*Inge Spurrell*
Bob Bishop	*Colin Dunster*	*Brian Kent*	*Raffaella St Clair*
C. Booth	*Brenda Durrant*	*Richard King*	*Harry Varden*
Simon Brocklehurst	*Peter Eddy*	*David Kirkham*	*Margaret Tidy*
Bill Broughton	*John Edwards*	*Patricia Knight*	*David Waine*
Mary Carpenter	*Pat Ferry*	*Tim Knight*	*A. & D. Wallace*
Chris Carpenter	*Ken Fidgen*	*Ruth Lambert*	*The Lord Walpole*
Philip Carter	*John Fish*	*Peter Lambert*	*Martin Warren*
Sandra & Keith Clark	*Nellie Fish*	*Chris Lewis*	*Richard Webster*
Gwen Coghlan	*Joan Fisher*	*Joan Long*	*Rosemary Webster*
John Cole	*Frances Glister*	*Joy Love*	*Peter Wedge*
Berti Cooke	*Carl Gray*	*Jane Maguire*	*Marion Wright*
Steve Cooke	*Cynthia Green*	*Gladys Miller*	*Alan Wright*
David Cooke	*Billy Hammond*	*Tom Mollard*	*Shirley Wright*
Jean Cooke	*Anne Hammond*	*Sue Mumford*	*Philip Wood*
Peter Crame	*Connie Harmer*	*John Neill*	
Robin Creasey	*Roy Harriss*	*Daphne Nichols*	
Betty & Roger Crouch	*J. & D. Haynes*	*Evelyn Peckham*	

We should also like to thank the following:

Churches Conservation Trust
Cromer Museum
Gressenhall Museum
Eastern Daily Press
Norfolk Record Office
Aldborough & Thurgarton Women's Institute

Bibliography

The WI History of Aldborough and Thurgarton
A beautiful work, handwritten by Mrs Phyllis Eddy. It has provided us with invaluable information on the parishes in the first forty years of the century. It is kept in the Norfolk Record Office.

All the works of the social historian **George Ewart Evans**, but two in particular: **The Farm and the Village** and **Where Beards Wag All**.

Penny Jackson's B.Ed. dissertation on Aldborough and Erpingham Primary schools

The splendid research material supplied by members of the Aldborough Village History Society Committee - Ruth Bayes, Ruth Elliott, Penny Jackson, Keith Good, Brian Metcalf, John Padgham.

Our thanks go to the copyright holders of George Barker's poem **At Thurgarton Church** for permission to include it in this volume.

We have made strenuous efforts to obtain permission from all holders of copyright for use in this book.